HOW NOT TO PULL YOUR FAMILY APART

A Practical Guide to Caregiving and Financial Stability

CARROLL S. GOLDEN

© 2022 Carroll S. Golden
All rights reserved.

No part of this publication in print, audible or in electronic format may be reproduced, stored in a retrieval system, or transmitted in any form or by any means, electronic, mechanical, photocopying, recording, or otherwise, without the prior written permission of the publisher.

The scanning, uploading, and distribution of this book without permission is a theft of the author's intellectual property. If you would like permission to use material from the book (other than for review purposes), please contact info@bublish.com. Thank you for your support of the author's rights.

Design and distribution by Bublish, Inc.

ISBN: 978-1-647046-41-5 (paperback)
ISBN: 978-1-647046-42-2 (eBook)

DEDICATION

This book is dedicated to my children, Erik and Nicole. My son and daughter never complain about the many hours that I spend working. They offer me constant encouragement, insight, and love. As a family, we believe that our tomorrows are filled with possibilities.

Heartfelt appreciation to my wonderful multi-generational family: Patty, Debbi, Vic, and Doug, for gracefully aging alongside me; my daughter-in-law Jodi; her parents, Carol and John; my grandchildren Carolyn and James, my nieces Lyndsey and Norah, and my great-nephew Colton, for their unreserved affection. As part of a multigenerational family, I gain insights into the many challenges families face planning for the physical, psychological, and financial demands that develop due to limited, extended, and long-term care needs.

ACKNOWLEDGMENTS

Thanks to my many personal and professional friends for their influence, sharing of knowledge, and inspiration. I am grateful to the leadership and participants of the Long Term Care Insurance Section of the Society of Actuaries and the Intercompany Long Term Care Insurance Conference and their sponsors for the many years of contributing and fostering a continual expansion of long-term care knowledge, innovation, and education.

I am grateful to the team at NAIFA and sponsors of the Limited and Extended Care Planning Center (LECP). The LECP Center strives to offer outstanding resources so advisors and consumers have access to actionable ideas and information.

I appreciate the collaboration and support offered by Angie Hughes, Sharon Reed, Steve Cain, Tom Riekse, Nicole Stuart, Erik Deer, Jodi Deer, Harlan Accola, Dan Mangus, Betty Meredith, and Joe Dowdall. Thank you for suggestions and reviewing sections of the book for accuracy and readability.

Special thanks to Suzanne Carawan for her inspiration and creativity, Byron Holz for his belief in my know-how, Jodi Deer and Nicole Stuart for their kindness in sharing their time and energy.

Without the generous guidance of Kathy Meis, my publisher, there would not be a book to share. Her continual encouragement, expertise, guidance, and her deep knowledge of the publishing industry were essential to bringing this story to life.

DISCLAIMER

Neither the author nor the other contributors offer this information as tax, legal, investment, retirement advice, or recommendations. The content is derived from sources believed to be accurate. Neither the information presented nor any opinion expressed constitute a solicitation for the purchase or sale of any product or security. Interpretation of planning tools and products is used in the context of the family story but may be suitable for other planning situations as well. Please consult an agent, investment advisor, tax consultant, or attorney before making a tax-related investment/insurance decision.

CONTENTS

Introduction xiii

SECTION I
HAVE THE CONVERSATION

Chapter 1   I Don't Want to Upset my Parents 3
Chapter 2   Get Ahead of the Curve 6
Chapter 3   How to Use This Book 8

SECTION II
PLAN, DON'T PANIC

Chapter 4   People Retire From Their Job But They Do Not
            Retire From Their Family 13
Chapter 5   An 'Unnamed' Phase of Retirement 15
Chapter 6   Treading Lightly and Acknowledging the Need
            for Generational Planning 18
Chapter 7   Setting up Communication Channels 23
Chapter 8   Step One: Create a Care Guide: A Window into
            the Past and a View of the Present 28
Chapter 9   Step Two: A Responsive Care Squad 36
Chapter 10 Step Three: Your Care Planning Team 41

Chapter 11	Figuring Out Today's and Tomorrow's Care Budget..... 46
Chapter 12	Family Forms A Dynamic Team 49
Chapter 13	Build a Knowledge Base about Long-Term Care Options 51
Chapter 14	What's the Deal with Medicaid and Medicare? 57
Chapter 15	The Home as a Funding Solution for Aging-in-Place 61
Chapter 16	Putting the Plan in Place: Multiple Options Fit the Bill! 65

SECTION III
A CAREGIVER'S LESSONS LEARNED

Chapter 17	The Sandwich Generation Issue Solved—Or is it? 69
Chapter 18	Retirement Planning is More Than a Simple Math Problem 76
Chapter 19	Step Two: Who is Available in Person or Virtually to Lend a Hand?... 80
Chapter 20	Expanding Beyond Family... 82
Chapter 21	Envisioning Your Future Self Through Self-Profiling ... 88
Chapter 22	Moving Your Extended or Long-Term Care Plan Forward 94

SECTION IV
FUNDING OPTIONS TO SUPPORT
FINANCIAL STABILITY

Chapter 23	A Health Savings Account as a Funding Mechanism.... 99
Chapter 24	What Are the Options for the Healthy and Not-So-Healthy?... 102
Chapter 25	The Pros and Cons of Traditional Long-Term Care 106
Chapter 26	Worksite Limited, Extended, and Long-Term Care..... 110

Chapter 27 Publicly Funded State Long-Term Care Programs 112
Chapter 28 Whole Life and Universal Life Insurance 115
Chapter 29 The Hybrid/Combo/Linked-Benefit Marketplace 117
Chapter 30 What Are Twofers and Double Twofers, and
            How Can They Help? 121
Chapter 31 Annuities with Riders 125
Chapter 32 Single Premium Immediate Annuity 128
Chapter 33 How Riders Can Help with Specific Care Needs 131
Chapter 34 Limited-Term Care Options 134
Chapter 35 Indemnity vs. Reimbursement Payouts 141
Chapter 36 Financial Wellness 143
Chapter 37 On Becoming an Educated Consumer 148
Chapter 38 Advisors as Moderators, Facilitators, or Mediators 151

Concluding Thoughts and Encouragement 155

INTRODUCTION

My History

I have been an advisor in the life and health-care industry for many years. After seeing how a lack of planning can destroy even the most stable of families, I decided to specialize in Long-Term Care. I discovered individuals do not define long term as an actual span of time but more by how well prepared the recipient and/or someone else is to recognize and manage care needs. Physical, emotional, and financial resources can quickly be exhausted. Stress can make a short amount of time feel like an eternity. I will use the terms extended or long-term care throughout this book because those terms accurately capture the reality of the need for multiple generations to plan for longer lives with growing psychological, financial, and health-care implications.

As a professional, I became more and more interested in long-term care by observing and experiencing families' multigenerational emotions collide with multigenerational logic. Investing in my professional growth, I enrolled in courses at the highly respected American College of Financial Services. I earned the Chartered Life Underwriter® (CLU®) and the Chartered Financial Consultant® (ChFC®) designations, which incorporate information and practical applications in the form of case studies around tax, retirement, and investment strategies. To increase my long-term care knowledge, I earned the Certification in Long-Term Care® (CLTC®) designation, which includes education in the fields of insurance, financial services, law, and accounting. Another specialized course, offered by America's Health Insurance Plans (AHIP), earned me the Long-Term Care Professional® (LTCP®) designation. Seeking to broaden my grasp of issues related to the "graying of America," I returned to the American College of Financial Services, where I earned the Chartered Advisor in Senior Living® (CASL®) designation, which is committed to helping aging clients achieve financial security now and into the future. While holding leadership positions in both major insurance companies and distribution agencies specializing in long-term care, I earned the Fellow, Life Management Institute® (FLMI®) designation, which is a ten-course professional development program that provides an industry-specific business education in the context of the insurance and financial services industry. Recently, I completed the Life and Annuity Certified Professional® (LACP®) designation from the National Association of Insurance and Financial Advisors (NAIFA), a certification that requires knowledge and experience beyond the requirements for industry licensure. Additionally, every two years I complete my state's continuing education licensure requirements, affording me the opportunity to learn and interact directly with consumers and advisors/agents.

I continue to gain insights from teaching, working, and holding leadership positions in professional associations. As a member of the Society of Financial Service Professionals (FSP), I served as a chapter president and taught continuing education (CE) classes. I was the chairperson for the Society of Actuaries® (SOA) Fifth Long-term Care Conference, and five years later, I chaired the Intercompany Long-Term Care Insurance Conference (ILTCI). As a speaker for the Retirement Speakers Bureau and for NAIFA's Limited and Extended Care Planning (LECP) Center, I enjoy offering interactive webinars on various extended and long-term care consumer planning options and retirement topics. I am responsible for creating and offering the Long-Term Care Insurance module for the Plan4Life/Salem University program, which leads to a professional certification as an Elder Planning Specialist. I serve as the executive director of NAIFA's Centers of Excellence, including the LECP Center. Supporters of NAIFA and the LECP Center represent different points in the continuum of care, but they share a common purpose and mission to maximize professional and consumer awareness and the distribution of limited and extended care solutions at a time when it is a growing generational American need.

I have two very smart sisters who are not close in age. Creating plans for them and their families meant learning to work with two different generations, both of whom were already busy with family, volunteer work, careers, and friends. It required me to broaden my familiarity with established and newer care options and to hone my ability to work with different budgets and different lifestyles.

My son and daughter reminded me about the shoemaker who had no shoes. I needed to plan for myself. I found myself working with yet another generation, and viewing life through their younger, simpler lens. It was and continues to be my most valuable lesson. From them, I learned the value of clear communication. Different generations attach different meanings to words and phrases. We all learn words and expressions in the context of our own experience, which may or may not be a shared experience.

As an employed caregiver to my daughter following an extensive operation which required a long healing process during which she could not walk, I was surprised to realize that I was living what I can only describe as a juggling act. Ultimately, I had to take a work-leave, move out of my home into my daughter's home, discontinue any social activities, and eventually experience physical and emotional exhaustion. The good news is the experience helped me create Jodi, the main character in this story.

My family's extended and long-term care planning provided me with a positive hands-on experience—and, just as significantly, the family situation into which I remarried provided me a more challenging experience, offering me psychological and financial insights. I know what you are thinking: "If you are so knowledgeable in this area, it must have been easy for you." It was informative but not easy. Additional lessons and insights were on the horizon. My in-laws had a history of both Alzheimer's disease and longevity in their gene pools. While advances in medicine and science have had a positive effect on longevity, diseases of the brain, unfortunately, have seen only marginal improvements. My husband's father suffered from Alzheimer's disease. Alzheimer's disease is the most common form of dementia. It causes problems with memory, thinking, and behavior. To varying degrees, he lost his ability to respond to his environment, remain in control of his movements, or carry on a conversation. The gene for Alzheimer's disease can be inherited. This scary thought exacerbated the difficulty of planning and made family conversations uncomfortable. Unspoken issues can be a communication stopper. We had to focus on options, including the possibility of the disease being passed on. On the other hand, my mother-in-law came from a family with a history of longevity, with relatives living well into their late nineties.

What is true for so many families was true for them. No one was comfortable starting the conversation. No one knew what to say or how to engage in an open dialogue. No one wanted to make our family's maturing members feel bad because of their potential care needs or feel like they were being punished for living a long life. No one wanted them to feel like they were being managed or handled. Maybe no one felt like they had the know-how to even find a suitable advisor or specialist. Or maybe they googled long-term care and became overwhelmed by everything that needed to be considered. No matter what caused the hesitation, it had a huge and very negative impact on my new family's finances and emotional cohesiveness. Discourse and disagreements about planning led to no planning. Later, when my mother-in-law needed care, the family could not agree on anything. The smallest decision led to awkward silences or nasty commentary.

I experienced firsthand how the lack of communication about family generational planning is exhausting, painful, and sad. I discovered many families mistakenly think that planning for care is unaffordable or would involve a long, drawn-out process.

How Can I Help You?

My mission is to demystify the limited, extended, and long-term care planning process and to provide actionable information you can use to help your family prepare for a financially stable future.

A major objective of my three step planning process is to establish an extended or long-term care plan to avoid counterproductive family stress or conflict. If you don't know how to talk with one another or if you don't know your options, you cannot see how to move forward. I'll provide an overview to broaden your familiarity with several options to fit almost any budget.

The industry's use of insurance lingo may cause you to back off a conversation about long term care. I have explained insurance and government program lingo in simple terms, but a deep dive with a professional is advised.

Families already come loaded with lots of built-in dynamics. We all know that too many players on a playing field creates confusion. My three steps create a game plan. All players are invited to the game, and everyone knows their role. Individual aptitudes, lifestyle demands, and availability are acknowledged. Just like a successful team, everyone in the family (however you define family) knows their role and respects others. After you engage in my simple three-step process, you will:

- Avoid singling out any family member or generation as "needy."
- Use this story book to start and continue the conversation about planning for the future.
- Use an inclusive rather than an exclusive approach, which means everyone feels good about, or at least accepts, the plan because they were part of the process.
- Establish leadership and rules so things move forward.
- Avoid having the financial burden fall on any one family member or friends.
- Avoid family members or friends feeling guilty because they can't interrupt their lives or live too far away to provide care.

- Become an educated consumer armed with relevant information and pertinent questions when consulting a professional.

During the COVID-19 pandemic, we saw two realities confirmed. First, no one is immune to sudden, unexpected care events. Second, most of us are unprepared for limited, extended, or long-term illness care needs. Leverage that learning! We all know that preparation is key and could have helped many families cope more effectively.

The goal of this book is to help individuals, families, and friends plan for both the expected and unexpected. Effort and courage are not enough without purpose and direction.

To bring to life the gravity of some issues facing families as they undertake this planning, I've created the Jones family, whose stories will hopefully demonstrate how all this works in the real world. There are three generations in the Jones family: the grandparents, James and Carolyn; their daughter and son-in-law, Jodi and Jackson; and their grandchildren, Erik and Nicole. You'll see yourself or someone you care about in these characters. Please share this book with your family members who need to understand what is at stake.

My three steps guide you in creating a Care Guide, a Care Squad, and a Care Planning Team. You establish a framework to start and continue conversations by opening lines of communication, encouraging participation, and talking about choices and financial stability.

The Care Guide is filled with relevant, accurate, and updated information. Each guide should contain a birthdate, height, weight, allergies, health conditions, medications (with dosages), primary language, passwords, emergency contacts, doctors' and specialists' contact information, and more. If a crisis occurs, no one has to scramble to find information because it's in the Care Guide. It's also a great planning tool. When planning, the more you know about the person you're helping, the better. Even if that person is you!

The objective of the Care Squad is to create a process for family members to react effectively when emergencies arise. It also provides a back-up plan in case the primary caregiver is not available.

The Care Planning Team (CPT) provides a structure for multigenerational discussions and assessments. The CPT discovers available options that suit each generation's immediate, extended, or long-term care needs. When it is time to seek professional advice or support, the CPT members are educated consumers—ready to discuss options, ask relevant questions, and make decisions!

This is about living your best possible life as you age and letting other generations do the same.

SECTION I

Have The Conversation

CHAPTER 1

I Don't Want to Upset my Parents

"Alone we can do so little, together we can do so much."

— *HELEN KELLER*

I was having a quick coffee with my friend, Rosa. She jumped when her cell phone rang. I saw the photo indicating that it was her mom calling. Her expression revealed tension and dismay. "It's my mom," she explained. "I am sure she needs something but I am not sure I can fit another thing into my day." Suddenly focusing on me, she apologetically said, "Sorry, did I say that out loud? That sounded so unkind."

Before she could continue, I reached over and squeezed her hand. "I know how much you love her. How can I help?" I asked.

"I can't even do some things my kids need me to do. I am becoming my friends worse nightmare. I depend on others for things I *want* to do with them." A tear rolled slowly down my friend's cheek. I felt her sadness.

Caring for her mom consumes most of Rosa's daily routine. She has lost sight of her true north and is now in survival mode, operating as if everything is a ten. She is her mother's sole caregiver. As the dementia worsens, prioritizing caregiving over her own health care needs, Rosa has delayed going to physical therapy for her hip discomfort despite worsening pain. She skipped scheduling a colonoscopy despite her father dying of colorectal cancer. We work together so I know she shows up to work looking exhausted and worried. She has taken so much time off that I wonder if she will just quit, or worse, lose her job.

Looking completely exhausted, Rosa squeezes my hand back, "I should have listened when you kept telling me to get a plan in place to handle some of these responsibilities but I was afraid of upsetting my Mom. All this running in circles is making me crazy. I am sure it has put my job in jeopardy and washed away any chance of my being in the promotion pipeline at work. I worry, constantly, that I'm not doing enough for my Mom and I know I'm not doing enough for my kids."

Despite my encouragement to plan for her parent's care, Rosa was worried it would upset her family if she talk about planning for her parent's care needs. Now, everything is upset.

Currently, many families both in the United States and abroad are caring for a parent while also caring for immediate family members and the generation beneath them. It's a natural life cycle. The term *sandwich generation* has been around for a long time, but comprehending its meaning is more important than ever with science and medical advances keeping us alive longer. This has put more adults with children *and* aging parents or close friends in the middle of a complicated juggling act.

When we think about our lifespan, we all hope to live a very long life. Rosa's lifespan may actually be shortened due to the intensity of caregiving she's providing for her parents.

Longevity intensifies the need to plan for extended or long-term care—and we're not just talking about health-care needs. There are also lifestyle needs and financial needs. Worrying about running out of money or being forced to move out of familiar surroundings is stressful. These issues affect a family's financial stability and relationships. The COVID-19 pandemic was a nasty wake-up call for the entire world. It opened all of our eyes to the limitations of the government, the health-care system, staffing issues, and even families' abilities to provide safe and adequate care when things go wrong at a local, state, national, or global level. If these realities aren't a trigger for you, then let me be clear: You need to have these important family conversations today and move toward a plan. The earlier you plan, the more options you have.

However you define family, unplanned limited, extended and long-term care issues can pull a family's financial stability and relationships apart. The only remedy is to plan; and the best plan is a result of becoming organized and educated about which options work best for your situation.

CHAPTER 2

Get Ahead of the Curve

> "Listening is power, listening to yourself is a superpower!"
>
> — SUKANT RATNAKAR

When you're reading the Jones family's story, you might be reminded of your own family or friends. Members of the Jones family have noticed the grandparents are showing signs of aging. They don't know how to start the awkward conversation about planning for the future as attitudes, beliefs, habits, experiences, values, and especially communication and comprehension differ from one generation to the next. However, the family uses the three steps outlined in this book to have "the talk" and navigate their options. This means they must work together as a team to address the many safety, health-care, financial, and lifestyle decisions ahead.

Is starting this important family conversation easy? No, it is not. It's difficult, but it is absolutely necessary. There are literally thousands, if not millions, of reports, disturbing statistics, and heartbreaking tales of financial ruin, generational infighting, and caregiver burnout that result from the lack of a plan. Unfortunately, the odds are stacked against you and time will not be on your side if you wait. For most families it takes a scary, sad, or upsetting experience to push everyone into action. By then, unfortunately, it's often too late to avoid some of the worst consequences of the family's delayed action. That's why it is so important to stay ahead of the curve. Without a plan, your family risks:

- Negative impacts on lifestyles. What if a parent must move in with you or if you must move in with a parent in need of care?
- Diminished Social Security benefits and retirement savings as the family caregiver devotes time to caregiving instead of earning income.
- Depletion of retirement savings.
- Delays in education funding for younger generations.
- On-the-job stress or employment absences due to caregiving requirements and emergencies.
- Decreased cash flow leading to limited care options.
- Diminished assets values resulting from a fire sale.
- Compelled asset liquidation when the market timing isn't good, resulting in unwanted taxation.
- Limited potential future investment growth due to diminished invested funds.
- Retirees and pre-retirees unable to preserve the money they have worked so hard to save.
- Feeling guilty because you didn't have the conversation with your parents or spouse, and their choices are unknown to you or are now less attractive or not possible.

You want a funded plan in place as early as possible so you can control the type of care, the care setting, and the care services for your future self or older family members. You also want these choices without breaking the bank.

CHAPTER 3

How to Use This Book

> "Fight for the things that you care about, but do it in a way that will lead others to join you."
>
> — *RUTH BADER GINSBERG*

Given the different stages of planning and different generational family compositions, it is best to modify/customize the information in this book according to your needs. These three steps—the book's foundation—can be used in any order. We will follow the Jones family as they customize the steps, and use the resources and tools to create a plan that fits their family's needs, budget, and goals. Here's a quick summary of the three steps.

Step One: Create a Care Guide: The "*I Care*" Conversation

Plan for immediate family care needs by creating a Care Guide filled with current, accurate information about each family member. The guide can be handed to doctors, health-care workers, and other service professionals in times of urgent need. Care Guides eliminate stress by consolidating and organizing crucial, up-to-date information. To avoid resistance to sharing personal information, the Care Guide can be a sealed document or on a password protected app. One significant resource that supports this proactive approach is PRISMM, www.getprismm.com, a cutting-edge digital vault designed for the secure storage of important documents. PRISMM's advanced privacy feature gives subscribers control over who can see what documents and when, thus ensuring a seamless and secure transfer of information. Caring actions speak louder than words.

Step Two: Select a Care Squad: The "*What If*" Conversation

The objective of the Care Squad is to create a process for family members to react effectively when emergencies arise. A Care Squad can help families avoid chaos and delays in a crisis situation. The Care Squad designates who does what when something goes wrong. Who goes over to Mom and/or Dad's house to be with them? Who calls the doctor or an ambulance? Who's in charge of handling the bills or interacting with insurers? Who contacts other family members or friends? You get the idea. Everyone knows their role in advance and can spring into action with a clear understanding of how they can help.

Step Three: Assign a Care Planning Team (CPT): The "*Discovery*" Conversation

The Care Planning Team (CPT) provides a structure for multigenerational discussions and assessments. CPT members each have a voice. As a group, they discover available options that suit each generation's immediate, extended, or long-term care needs. The generational diversity of the group should encourage and require respect and acknowledgement of different lifestyles and generational priorities. When it is time to seek professional advice or support, the CPT members are educated consumers—ready to discuss options, ask relevant questions, and make decisions!

These three steps are achievable. They provide a gateway to important conversations that are often hard to start, but are always better to have before a crisis hits. Even though the Jones family is fictitious, these scenarios play out every day. Hopefully, seeing the Jones family work through their issues, choices, and roadblocks will inspire you and give you courage to take the first step towards planning with multigenerational family members and/or friends. Products and services may apply differently to your situation, but this story should increase your familiarity with the available options and move you to action. Knowledge is a powerful tool.

SECTION II

Plan, Don't Panic

CHAPTER 4

People Retire From Their Job But They Do Not Retire From Their Family

> "Family is not an important thing, it's everything."
>
> — MICHAEL J. FOX

Traditionally, retirement meant leaving a nine to five job and living out your golden years. Social security income and pensions supported retiree's lifestyles. By the end of the twentieth century, life expectancy had reached seventy-seven years. This increase in life expectancy has made caring for older family and friends more common.

Born between 1928 and 1945, the silent generation were children of the Great Depression. They kept their heads down and worked hard, thus earning themselves the silent label. They were not risk-takers and played it safe.

Meet the oldest generation of the Jones Family. Grandpa James and Grandma Carolyn Jones are part of the silent generation which has shaped their value system and lifestyle predilection. As we will see, different generational imprints influence the conversations and ideas right from the outset in the Jones family. Typical of their generation, retirees Grandpa James and Grandma Carolyn expect Social Security income and company pensions to be a major source of retirement income. Like many older adults, they assume their children will eventually be their caregiver. However, if asked, Grandpa James feels he can take care of Grandma Carolyn.

Historically, housing designs did not, and many still do not, consider the aging process. At one point, adding an in-law suite or granny flat became popular. However, aging parents living with their adult children and/or grandchildren creates an array of family dynamics as care needs evolve.

Additionally, today's generations are increasingly mobile, and distant caregiving is complicated. Yet, many children must take on the role of a caregiver, acting as information coordinators, helping aging parents understand the confusing maze of new needs and finding affordable services. Do you see yourself in that role? Without a plan you may already be the presumptive generational caregiver. The first frank conversation you need to have is with yourself is what can you do, and what can you not do?

CHAPTER 5

An 'Unnamed' Phase of Retirement

> "You may not control all the events that happen to you, but you can decide not to be reduced by them"
>
> — MAYA ANGELOU

As we move through life stages, family members (however you define family) take care of one another. It's what family is all about. Over the years and through the decades we accept, prepare, and plan for the next life-stage.

Nowadays, retirement can refer to a period that may stretch out twenty or thirty years. We lack a phrase to describe the later phase when retirement years morph into interdependency and require increasing levels of assistance. Logically, retirement preparation should include preparing for long-term care needs. But few people prepare. Somehow this topic throws us for a loop.

We fail to plan for the inevitable: Mom and Dad will age, will probably live much longer than their parents did, and will probably require more specialized care over a longer period. More family caregivers are in the workforce—currently, some sixty percent work full- or part-time. This trend will continue, and those who have to pull back during their working years face substantial economic risk from loss of income, benefits, contributions to their own retirement savings, or reduced Social Security benefits.

Let's check in on the Jones family to see how they handle some changes they're seeing.

The Jones family plans their annual get-together to celebrate Grandma Carolyn's seventy-sixth birthday on Zoom. All four generations of the Jones family attend. Everyone enjoys the party, but they quietly notice Grandma Carolyn's increasing frailty. Grandpa James has to help her stand up to blow out the candles on her birthday cake. Everything seems to move in slow motion and everyone leaves the Zoom call concerned about Grandma Carolyn.

Grandma's daughter, Jodi, is especially dismayed by what she has seen. Over the last year, she has gradually taken on more and more caregiver duties, such as shopping, preparing meals, driving her parents to appointment that involve heavily trafficked or high-speed roads, speaking with doctors about treatments, running errands, doing laundry, and changing bed linens. It's been a gradual process. As a result, she doesn't really even associate all she is doing with caregiving. Her father, James, always offers to help, but with his pacemaker and family history of heart failure, Jodi typically politely refuses.

Jodi's husband and two children see how each new responsibility takes its toll on Jodi. Sleep deprivation, unhealthy eating habits, and lack of exercise are just a few of the signs of her stress and overburdened schedule. After the birthday party, they fear things will get worse. Jodi's daughter, Nicole, even suspects there have been financial consequences her mom hasn't mentioned. She and her brother Erik talk and decide to take action before things get worse. Erik prints a copy of an article to use as a jumping off point for a conversation about planning for long-term care. They call their dad, Jackson, for advice. He explains the topic is sort of taboo, but he knows he needs to approach Jodi to start the conversation.

It's a typical situation. The grandparents have no plan in place, at least not one the family knows about. What often happens without a plan is the care is self-funded by the senior and/or their spouse or partner until most or all assets are depleted. At that time, the person needing care may qualify for Medicaid, which is far from an optimal solution, or family members must dip into their own funds to pay for needed care. Knowing how to finance extended care is essential, but it is obviously not the only issue.

Everyone, as they notice the effects of growing older, would prefer not to leave familiar surroundings. It's where most of us want to be—at home. But what if the home requires a variety of costly and disruptive renovations? What about upkeep and socialization? All these considerations can be researched and decided only once critical conversations get started.

What about the personal side of needing or providing care? More than twenty-five percent of seniors who need long-term care are incapable of making their own decisions when the time comes. Making those decisions for someone you love or are responsible for is an emotional burden family members find extremely difficult. The impact of those decisions can linger for many years and often leads to family conflict.

If you do not move forward with planning, many of these difficult, long-lasting consequences will become a part of your family's history. With our care plans in place, I see how confident my sisters, brothers-in-law, and our children are that our immediate family was and will be cared for without unduly burdening family members.

It's a conversation about how to *help*, instead of how to *handle* someone. It is hard to see a loved one lose their vitality, but it is unbearable to know you could have made the aging and care process more comfortable by planning but didn't get around to it!

CHAPTER 6

Treading Lightly and Acknowledging the Need for Generational Planning

> "We delight in the beauty of the butterfly, but rarely admit the changes it has gone through to achieve that beauty"
>
> — MAYA ANGELOU

Due to COVID-19 restrictions, the Jones family hadn't seen the cumulative effect aging is having on Grandma Carolyn. The Zoom get-together shook them up. Everyone is now acknowledging that a conversation is needed, except the caregiver Jodi. Caregivers often don't seek help until they become overwhelmed.

Jackson, as promised, brings up the topic with his wife. They sit down at the kitchen table to discuss if they should involve their entire family in the long-term care planning process.

"I know the kids want to help," Jodi explains, "but I can handle it."

"Jodi, I understand you want to shelter them, but they are family. They want to help. I'm not sure excluding them is the best course of action. I was reading about this in the news the other day. We're typical of the sandwich generation, caring for three generations at the same time—your parents, ourselves, and our children. You know how financially savvy Nicole is. Well, she sent me an article about the impact all of this could have on our retirement. It wasn't pretty, and she hesitated to send it to you."

"Why?" Jodi looks inquisitively at her husband.

"She doesn't want to upset you. She doesn't want you to think she's meddling," Jackson responds, placing his hand on his wife's arm. "Jodi, this is impacting everyone. Not saying anything to our children just makes them worry even more."

"OK," Jodi stiffens while trying not to sound defensive. "Please show me what she sent."

Jackson nudges the article toward his wife. "I know Nicole shared it with Erik. According to the Fidelity Retiree Health Care Cost Estimate, a couple aged sixty-five who retired back in 2020 needed approximately $295,000 saved after taxes to cover health-care expenses in retirement. For affluent investors, that number could rise to $320,000 or more depending on state taxes. The article warns that many people assume Medicare will cover all health-care costs in retirement, but apparently it doesn't. This chart illustrates that about fifteen percent of the average retiree's annual expenses will be used for health care–related expenses. It's a pretty eye-opening article, Jodi."

Impacts of Medical Expenses on Retirement

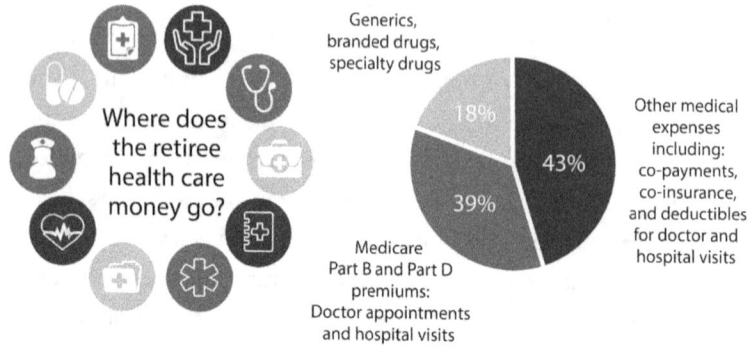

How to plan for rising health care costs Estimated cost for health care post-age 65? Try $295,000 per couple in assets needed today.
Fidelity Viewpoints 08/03/2020 https://www.fidelity.com/viewpoints/personal-finance/plan-for-rising-health-care-costs accessed 10/10/2020

"I had no idea." Jodi leans in with a concerned look on her face. "That's a big chunk of money."

"Exactly." Jackson nods. "Can you imagine if our own health deteriorates or if we simply have the good fortune, like your parents, to live long enough to experience the effects of getting older and then cause this same concern for our children?"

"Yeah," Jodi agrees, "everyone hopes to live a long and healthy life, but it looks like it's going to take some additional planning to stretch our nest egg."

"Honey, Erik and I have been discussing his ability to save for retirement. Since his wife isn't working right now so she can take care of their young kids, it might be tough for a while." Jackson places another article on the table in front of Jodi. "He shared this with me; the kids suspect you didn't take that promotion because you want more time to help your parents. The article says family caregivers who disrupt their careers or leave the labor force entirely to meet caregiving demands can face substantial economic risk and both short- and long-term financial difficulties."

Jackson and Jodi sit quietly at the table consumed by their thoughts and dreading what lies ahead.

So many of us are like the Jones family. We don't know how to frame the conversation, we don't know the next steps, and we certainly don't have a plan to deal with what's coming.

Luckily, after listening to her husband and hearing how concerned her children are, Jodi acknowledges it is time for the family to navigate a workable plan. She decides to visit her parents for an initial conversation and then schedule a Zoom call with everyone to discuss the next steps. After visiting her parents, Jodi tells Jackson she understands the need to include the entire family in the conversation, but it didn't go well with her father. "He went between pretending that nothing is wrong and insinuating that I don't want to help them."

Jackson comforts his wife and waits until she is ready to continue the conversation.

"Look Jackson, I know you and the kids are right," she says, and her expression shows exhaustion and resignation, "but my dad looked at me as if I wanted to take over his life. I felt guilty just bringing it up. Maybe we should wait and just let him get used to the idea."

"He will never get used to the idea, Jodi," Jackson flatly responds. "We need to explain to your parents we are all doing the care guides and other steps to form a plan, not a punishment. You need to arrange a Zoom call and include both your parents."

Jodi becomes more anxious. "What if he won't join? We need to include my father since there is no point in making decisions or proposing ideas unless he agrees."

"Then explain that we are doing a family project." Jackson holds his wife, who begins to softly cry. "Don't worry, honey. I know you're overwhelmed, but we'll figure this out."

"I know you're right, Jackson. I just feel pulled in so many directions. I feel like I am failing everyone. And I'm so tired."

The reality is that family conversations about the implications of extended care planning are taxing and challenging. But the stakes are very high.

Will Jodi be a caregiver who ends up providing care that takes her away from spending time with her children and grandchildren? Will she know if her parents are victims of lottery scams or online fraud? Will they be among adults who say they are willing or want to talk about their end-of-life wishes but don't have a way to do so? Poor family planning creates emergencies. Jodi has been aware of her mother's growing unsteadiness. This lack of planning often creates two difficult conversations, one with an aging adult and a second one with a caregiver in denial.

CHAPTER 7

Setting up Communication Channels

> "The difference between misery and happiness depends on what we do with our attention"
>
> — *SHARON SALZBERG*

Good communication is the key to success in any undertaking but especially when dealing across generations. Care options that work for one generation may be uncomfortable or unaffordable for another. The Jones family is typical of veiled generational challenges.

Jackson arranges a Zoom call with Erik and Nicole. He arranges for Jodi's parents to join later so he can bring his children up to speed first.

"Mom visited with Grandma and Grandpa. We're all now aware that Grandma Carolyn has become less steady on her feet. Your mom has been dealing with it for some time. Your grandparents will join the call in a few minutes, and we want to be careful to respect they may not immediately warm to the idea of us arranging a plan for their future care. Keep that in mind and let's all remember we have one mouth and two ears for a reason!"

Just then, Jodi interrupts. "Oh, Grandpa is in the waiting room. I'll admit him."

Warm greetings are shared, and Grandpa James announces Grandma will not be joining. Already very concerned about Grandma, everyone carefully maintains their warm expressions.

Jodi breaks the silence. "Dad, the other day, you and I discussed if we should ask Grandma's doctor if she should get a cane to steady her up. I did some research and, frankly, I'm alarmed to learn that statistically, when an elderly person falls, their hospital stays are almost two times longer than those of elderly patients who are admitted for any other reason. Sadly, according to the Center for Disease Control and Prevention (CDC), falls are the leading cause of death from injury among people age sixty-five and older with more than half of all injury-related deaths involving people age seventy-five or over."

Grandpa James, looking concerned, takes a moment to internalize the information. "I had no idea. For Grandma, the most profound effect of falling would be the loss of her ability to function independently." Chuckling, he adds, "Or her version of independently."

Wanting to appear supportive of Grandpa's attempt at humor, the family members nod or smile, but it is easy to read their faces, which clearly indicate they fear their grandma is at risk of adding to those scary statistics.

Jodi decides this is her opportunity to be more open with her dad. "And as long as we are discussing this together, let me share that Jackson and I are equally concerned about the effects Grandma's unsteadiness could have on you, both emotionally and physically, Dad."

Jodi's son, Erik, seizes the opportunity to add, "OK, while we are adding concerns about the effects on Grandma and Grandpa, we should also discuss the effects it is having on you, Mom."

"Oh, right, yes, that," Jodi stumbles along in response. "I saw the research you and Nicole did on your own concerning the effects of caregiving on the caregiver." Worried that this acknowledgment will upset her father, she hurriedly adds, "However, let's all agree that we need, as a family, to focus on caring for Grandma first. We do not want to wait until Grandma's unsteadiness turns into an emergency."

"Especially with all of us still working," Erik says. As an afterthought he asks, "Who'd take care of her?"

"I'd take care of her," Grandpa firmly announces, revealing his affection for his wife and his obvious intention to stay in control. Jodi may be the family matriarch, but Grandpa James certainly sees himself as fiercely independent and as head of his household.

Jodi is alarmed at her father's defensive attitude. "Dad, can you agree, as remote a chance as it, that it's possible you might not be able to take care of Mom as you would wish?" Clearly, her father is struggling with the idea of where this planning meeting is heading. Hoping to reestablish a caring and open atmosphere, Jodi adds, "That is why we're all on this call; to work together to prepare for the unexpected."

Tensions are surfacing, so the Jones family will have to move forward and foster a level of cooperation. Planning for care is a multilayered process.

Grandpa James is aware of the toll that helping him and Grandma Carolyn has taken on his daughter. He knows she has taken time off from work and passed up a promotion. He has seen what a roller coaster of emotions it has been for both his daughter and his son-in-law. He also suspects Jodi has put funds aside in case she needs to pay for services or provide other financial assistance. He read an article about the effect it would have on his daughter's retirement if she continues to help them. It saddens him, but until now, he really didn't know what to do about it. Hard as it will be, he agrees to participate in the process since Jodi said it is a just-in-case scenario and it is a family project.

Grandpa James closes the call with a smile, saying, "OK, looks like a family project, but let's not get carried away. What do you have in mind as a potential solution?" He sees both relief and concern spread over the faces of the others. He experiences a flood of mixed emotions, but is determined to appear to be supportive—provided he approves of this plan!

We know Grandpa James is not necessarily on the same page as the rest of the family. My three steps provide an organized way to work toward a solution. The steps are a natural progression, similar to what we see during a home renovation. The home represents a family's history and emotional ties for multiple generations. During the home renovation design phase, family values, dreams, and wishes come to light. As things progress, decisions are made based on what is possible since not every wish can become a reality. Similarly, the reality of planning for a family's eventual need for limited, extended, or long-term care initially involves gathering wishes which will need to be tempered by factual realties.

Next, construction on the home begins and inevitably challenges arise. Challenges are overcome by having the right person in the right role. Compromises must be made based on feasible options, priorities, and practicalities, so the team must work together. In the end, the family, designers, and workers are pretty happy with the results of the planned renovation. For each renovation, the overall process is the same, but the outcomes vary by family needs and resources. In a nutshell, they used a process. The Jones family, like most, need a process that leads to accomplishing their goal. And like the home renovation team, both planners and recipients will have to prioritize must haves over nice to haves, gather information, examine options, assign roles, and accept modifications and changes along the way. The three steps provide an *inclusive* rather than *exclusive* approach, with the goal of creating an effective plan.

CHAPTER 8

Step One: Create a Care Guide: A Window into the Past and a View of the Present

> "Most of the shadows of this life are caused by standing in our own sunshine."
>
> — RALPH WALDO EMERSON

Getting organized is not everyone's strong suit. Here is a helpful list of some basic elements for a Care Guide.

HOW NOT TO PULL YOUR FAMILY APART

The Care Guide

This list includes but is not limited to the following suggestions:

01 ▶ Basic Questionnaire

- (1) Health History
- (2) Allergies
- (3) Family Health History
- (4) Primary Language
- (5) Prior Hospital Stays
- (6) Travel Exposures
- (7) Medications (Prescribed)
- (8) Implanted Devices
- (9) Medications (Over the Counter)
- (10) Hearing & Vision Details
- (11) Chronic Condition(s)
- (12) Dental Needs

02 ▶ Professional Contacts Questionnaire

- (1) Doctors
- (2) Specialists
- (3) CPA or Tax Advisors
- (4) Investment Advisor
- (5) Attorney
- (6) Insurance Advisor/Agents

03 ▶ Financial Worksheet

- (1) Investments
- (2) Insurances
- (3) Savings
- (4) Debts
- (5) Property
- (6) Other Assets/Liabilities

04 ▶ Wishes of Care Recipient - Questionnaire / Document

1. Collaborative Care Plan
2. Alignment of Treatment Plan with Patient Goals
3. Personal Letter(s) Written by Care Recipient
4. Distribution of Personal Assets or Belongings

05 ▶ Communication Contact Questionnaire - Personal & Family Information Form

1. Personal
2. Family
3. Friends
4. Professional

06 ▶ Legal Questionnaire

1. Last Will and Testament
2. Living Trust
3. Directives
4. Contracts
5. Beneficiary Documents
6. Trusts

07 ▶ Government Programs

1. Medicare Eligibility
2. Medicaid Eligibility
3. Coverage and Services
4. Liens and Third Party Liability (other Insurance)
5. Provider Enrollment
6. Claims
7. Lost Medicaid Card/ Replacement
8. Veteran Questionnaire

HOW NOT TO PULL YOUR FAMILY APART

08 ▶ Caregiver Facility or Agency Document

1. Contact Information
2. Employee/Caregiver Background Check Policy
3. Service Start Dates
4. Termination Clause
5. List of Caregiving Services
6. Frequency of Service
7. Financial Obligation
8. Backup Plan for Caretaker Absence

09 ▶ Contract with Independent Caregiver

1. Contact Information
2. Location(s)
3. Start Dates and Hours
4. Define Key Service Levels
5. Define Liability Between Each Party
6. List All Obligations and Record Keeping
7. Backup Plan for Caretaker Absence
8. Modification/Termination Clause
9. Signed by Care Recipient and the Caregiver
10. Have the Document Notarized

10 ▶ Retirement Budget Worksheet

1. Contact Information
2. Financial Statements
3. Goals
4. Income/Savings
5. Expenses/Subscriptions/Reoccurring Payments
6. Donations/Debts/Insurances

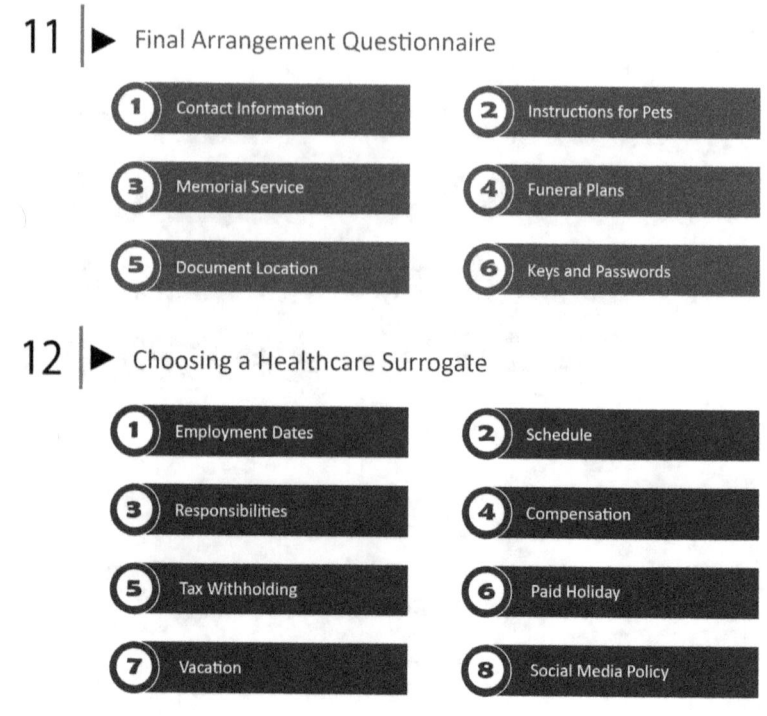

Typical of most families, each person in the Jones family has seen or heard something about Grandpa James and Grandma Carolyn's medical or financial information. But does anyone know where various documents are kept? Is it in a vault at their bank that only they can access? Are there important documents that have been lost or were never executed? Are they kept on a computer with an undisclosed password? In order to be ready for an emergency and extended care planning, the Jones family needs to centralize important information and fill in the blanks. Importantly, they will be released from carrying the burden of whether or not they made the right decisions.

During the family's next Zoom gathering, Jodi observes everyone is participating in the conversation. The initial awkwardness seems to be fading and conversations are becoming more productive. Jodi outlines the three steps. Her dad seems OK with everything so far.

Jackson, actively supportive, offers an agenda to start the call. "We need to gather and organize information and see which, if any, important documents are missing. While we are helping Grandma and Grandpa get organized, let me also say that this is something we should all prepare for each member of our families. None of us is getting any younger. Aging and accidents happen! It's important to be prepared."

Jodi shoots Jackson a look signaling him to stay focused on Grandma and Grandpa.

"But today, we are following a generational order so our focus is Grandpa and Grandma," Jackson refocuses. "First, we need to decide who will handle organizing the documentation."

"I will," Nicole volunteers. "I'll create a spreadsheet with different categories like health history, medications, insurance, documents, and so forth. I'll make sure to add the contact information for their doctors, accountants, and lawyers."

"Nicole, you're so sweet," Grandpa James says adoringly, "but I know you are very busy at work."

Jackson thinks but doesn't say out loud, "Uh oh, here we go!"

"Don't worry, Grandpa, you and Grandma are my favorite project." Nicole blows her grandfather a kiss through her iPad.

"Thank you, Nicole, but we don't want to be a burden. Why don't I just write everything out that you need to know."

Sensing her grandpa's reluctance and reacting to the word burden, Nicole decides to be direct. "We're not trying to be nosy. We're trying to keep you safe."

"I understand, sweetheart, and I don't want to seem defensive, but there's certain information that Grandma and I feel is for our eyes only. You know, we've been doing OK handling this all by ourselves for a very long time."

"Yes, you have, and I respect that, Grandpa." Nicole leans in, picking up on Grandpa's need to remain in control. "Sharing the information will allow us to respect your wishes and not make decisions without your guidance. What if it's you who falls and gets injured? Do you think it will upset Grandma if she doesn't know how to handle it and we don't have the information to be helpful? Can you imagine how she would feel? We don't want her, or you, to become a statistic. We are your family. We care and we want to help. What if we do this together, Grandpa—just the two of us? I will respect that it isn't mine to share."

Grandpa is shaken by the reality of Nicole's questions. He faintly smiles and nods. "OK, um, you might be right," he says and thinks, and this way if something does happen, you won't need to go through our belongings to find what you need.

Thinking back to the statistics his mother shared about falls, Erik weighs in. "Let's start by organizing the information we need to handle any immediate needs that might arise."

The Jones family has navigated the first steps in creating a Care Guide for Grandpa and Grandma and addressed Grandpa's concerns about privacy and control.

A quick review of current documents, such as end-of-life wishes, wills, health care proxy, and do-not resuscitate orders indicate the grandparents should immediately take care of important legal documents. They would be well advised to update their will and create legal medical directives. Family and/or close friends prefer to *know* someone's wishes in case of illness, mental incapacity, or a prolonged inability to properly make health-care decisions. Each state has specific regulations and forms available for use. If done correctly, these directives and documents save the family, friends, and professionals a great deal of difficulty and angst by providing guidance. If someone changes their state of residency, it is important to see if new documents are needed. While there are sites that offer free document forms, the Jones family accessed a helpful site, www.naela.org, to identify and locate elder and special needs law attorneys. The site is searchable by attorney name, practice area, language, or zip code.

Once the documents and directives are in good order, duplicates will be added to the grandparents' Care Guide. This important step adds to everyone's peace of mind.

The next step is to create a Care Squad to help manage the response in a family emergency. Step Two comes with its own challenges and opportunities. Step One—the Care Guide—is about coming together, organizing, and opening lines of communication. Step Two—the Care Squad—is about creating an action plan and assigning people to each role in that plan. Currently, all roles fall on Jodi's shoulders. She is a pretty typical caregiver, and more and more of us are finding ourselves in that role.

CHAPTER 9

Step Two: A Responsive Care Squad

> "Perhaps the greatest test of love is the way we act in times of need."
>
> — SULEIKA JAOUAD

According to a November 2019 AARP Public Policy Institute report, back in 2017, about million unpaid family caregivers provided an estimated thirty-four billion hours of care—worth 470 billion dollars—to their parents, spouses, partners, and friends.

As a nation, we need to stop pushing this issue to the back burner. There are simply not enough trained caregivers and staff to take care of everyone who will need assistance. More and more of us will be obligated to take on a role for which few of us are trained. Caregiving is often a progressive role:

- the "on call" caregiver offers incidental help, phone calls to check-in, and errand assistance.

- the "on-site" caregiver sees incidental help morph into more and more obligations, handling doctor visits, cooking, shopping, general housekeeping, and personal needs.
- the "on-the-side" caregiver must jump in when the on-call or on-site caregiver is unavailable or overwhelmed. Not knowing the routine, it's not an easy role.
- the "on-a-flight" caregiver may incur costly distant travel and time away from work and personal obligations.

Creating a Care Squad is a simple but effective step for being inclusive while organizing limited resources. Start with tasks that fit easily into a Care Squad member's current lifestyle or capability. If you are the on-a-flight caregiver but can review bills, that's perfect. If you can help with on-call needs such as being available to drive to doctor appointments, volunteer for that. If you are on-the-side but can review technology options as an aid to aging-in-place, take on that role. If you live close by, volunteer to grab the Care Guide in an emergency. Find things that work easiest or best with current availability and only then move on to things that might be more of an infringement on an individual's schedule.

Assigned roles help to minimize chaos and hysteria. Finally, knowing they are part of the family Care Squad, family members or friends feel less helpless or discounted.

Let's see how the generational Jones family handle Step Two.

Jodi kicks off the next meeting on a positive note. "I want to thank all of you for pitching in and getting Step One done!"

The family seems pleased with themselves and the relief on Jodi's face is truly a pleasure to see.

"Now, let's get started with Step Two," she continues. "In an emergency or when a plan for long-term care is needed, we have all seen responses that are frantic, emotional, unorganized, or disjointed."

"You should hear some of the horror stories my friends share with Grandma and me," Grandpa James says. "Our neighbor Sharon was rushed to the hospital. When they allowed her kids into her room, she said the tension took all the air out of the room. Then they started arguing over who would do what, along with who should have done what. She felt like all the snarling and tense exchanges were all her fault. What a nightmare!"

Thrown off balance by her father's narrative, Jodi regains her composure. "In order to avoid stress-related reactions like grandpa just described, we will create a Care Squad. This step is not complicated, but it is very effective. One recommendation I have for assigning responsibilities is to start with basic tasks that fit easily into our current lifestyles and then add as needed. Here is a simple diagram that I found on that we can fill in based on everyone's availability and comfort level."

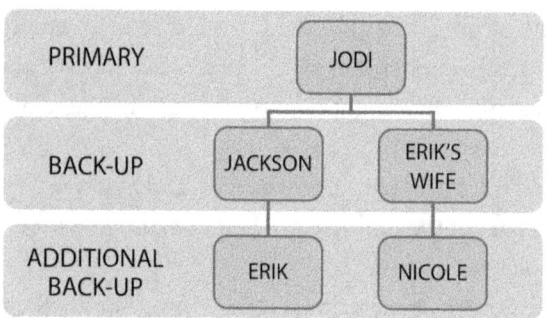

The Jones family has made good progress. Before they can move on to Step Three, there's an emergency. We get to see Steps One and Two in action.

Jodi and Jackson take Jodi's parents over to visit Erik, his wife, and their young children. Happy to have all four generations together, the family sets up chairs outside in the yard. The ground outside is not as level as inside, so Grandma Carolyn's and Grandpa James's chairs are placed on the driveway. Grandma, a bit unsteady on her feet, tries to get up and starts to fall. Grandpa, sitting next to her, tries to break her fall. They both tumble onto the hard surface of the driveway.

Grandma is in a good deal of pain. Grandpa seems to have broken his wrist. Both are very pale, and Grandma has tears in her eyes. Jodi looks very shaken up. Erik's young children start to cry. While a perfect scenario for chaos, Jackson reminds them of their assignments. With a role to focus on, they quickly get organized.

The grandparents, in pain and pretty unhappy, will not have to be further upset by trying to remember essential details and documented information since they each have a Care Guide. The three generations pull together and avoid the additional anxiety that comes with facing sudden and unexpected care events.

Once they are back home, Jodi turns to her husband. Expecting a flood of tears, Jackson is surprised to see Jodi composed.

Jodi remarks, "Well, that went better than I would ever have expected! Everyone seemed to act with a purpose instead of overdoing it! With Nicole getting and delivering the Care Guide, calling her brother to keep him informed, then bringing us coffee, I could concentrate on supporting Mom and Dad. The emergency room took the documents, which helped speed us through the check-in process. Remember last time when we waited and waited while they waited for current documents and information? I saw my dad's face when the attending physician complimented us for being prepared. He assured my parents that with their Care Guide in hand he could confidently and more quickly move forward with his assessment and suggested treatment. Although they were in pain, they seemed less scared since the process was moving along pretty smoothly."

Jackson opened his mouth, shut it, and instead just smiled, nodding his head in agreement. Hating to diminish Jodi's positive assessment, he still felt obligated to add, "Honey, I think we had better move on to Step Three. Your mom is probably not going to recovery too quickly. You dad will have his cast on for a while. They need a long-term care plan."

"Absolutely, Jackson. Too bad we did not get through that last step before this happened."

Younger generations and families without relatives living nearby may form a Care Squad made up of close friends or neighbors. You may want to share the Care Guide in a sealed envelope or give them access to an online vault.

CHAPTER 10

Step Three: Your Care Planning Team

> "All journeys have secret destinations of which the traveler is unaware."
>
> — *MARTIN BUBER*

The driveway incident was a harsh wake-up call for the Jones family. Many of us can relate. Once the grandparents are released from the hospital, ongoing care will be required. It is a harbinger of future care needs.

Now that the emergency has passed, members of the Jones family need to return to their own lives, but they also know they need to figure out the right option for long-term care needs. This is the primary objective of the Care Planning Team (CPT).

The first issue is, who should be invited to participate in a Care Planning Team? The Jones family includes three adult generations, all of whom are absorbed by their own busy lives. Nicole is very engaged in her career; Erik is the sole supporter of his family; Jodi is already busy supervising her mother's recovery, settling her father into a new routine, and trying to keep her job (she has given up the idea of a qualifying for any promotion); and Jackson, working full time, has concerns about his own parents, who are needing some guidance and help. In addition, getting Grandpa to cooperate is still a challenge. Let's see how they handle it.

"Well, we dodged that bullet." Jodi says, sitting at home with Jackson. She still isn't fully recovered from the bad fright of what happened to her parents. Her initial reaction, appreciating the effectiveness of Steps One and Two, has given way to the looming reality of having her mother discharged from the hospital. "Mom is doing OK but has a pretty intense recovery road ahead of her. After broken bones knit, there will be physical therapy. Dad has a cast that I am sure he will have the kids sign!" She nervously laughs.

Jackson replies, "Thank goodness for the first two steps so we were better prepared to actively help." Reaching over, Jackson puts his hand gently on his wife's shoulder. "Honey, I hope you agree there is no way you can be the only one helping your parents as they heal. We will now certainly have to get them some in-home help and start into Step Three."

"I know, I know!" Jodi says rubbing her temples. "I worry they will reject the idea as an invasion of their privacy, not talk about it, and just try to handle things on their own."

Seeing his wife so tense and worried, Jackson flatly states, "Well, that's not realistic. Plus, your Mom is showing signs of confusion." Quickly he adds, "Hopefully, it's the result of her medications." Jackson immediately regrets his remark.

Jodi and Jackson have an advisor whose father suffers from Alzheimer's Disease. Fortunately, the advisor's sister was a nurse and handled their dad. But Alzheimer's patients require more care and supervision than can generally be handled at home, so eventually they found a facility for him. After he was settled in, which was a struggle since change is often very difficult for

Alzheimer's patients, he had a health incident that caused him to be admitted to the hospital. They lost the bed in the facility. They had to keep their dad in the hospital much longer than needed until they finally found another facility that would take him and accommodate his needs. It wasn't conveniently located for either one of his children. Plus, changing his facility again was unsettling for him, and them.

Wanting to move on, Jackson says, "Honey, let's get your father and the kids to form the Care Planning Team and start the discovery process. It would allow us to work together to investigate, research, and work with agents, advisors, or specialists to secure a viable plan."

In establishing the CPT, be as inclusive as possible. Exclusivity can stir up a family feud. Let me share a personal story. It was a tough lesson. My husband's parents nominated their older son, my husband, as their executor. They didn't include their younger son in the planning process. My husband's father passed away, leaving the two sons to care for their mother. During the time that their mother lived in an assisted living facility and later when she was required to move into the nursing home wing of the facility, the two brothers continually argued about details for their mother's care, what facility was best, and all sorts of related cost of care issues. Emotions run high when dealing with someone else's care; love, guilt, hope, fear, confusion, worry, and a myriad of other emotions can often manifest into a family feud and pull generations apart. To this day, the brothers do not speak to each other or their wives and children. It is and remains a divided family. I am sure it isn't what his parents would have wanted.

I am certain that if we had created a CPT, they may have argued, but both brothers and their families would have felt heard and would forcibly have worked toward a compromise. Not inviting a family member (or close friend where appropriate) to be part of the CPT is the same as excluding them. Explain the role and time commitment. If they cannot find the time to participate in the CPT, it is wise to let them indicate as much. If they decide to drop out during the process, you still are not the one who excluded them.

In my experience, since not every family member may be as cooperative as one might hope, the CPT must establish some commonsense rules. Each individual and each generation has its own vocabulary and is influenced by its own lifestyle, value system, and maturity level. The CPT may have to establish what is on the table and what is off the table. Being included in the CPT is not a license to be intrusive. Be inclusive but not naïve. Establish some rules. In the absence of a natural leader, consider an advisor as a facilitator or mediator so the planning process doesn't stall.

Let's see how the Jones family worked out this new challenge.

"OK," Jodi concedes as they discuss the Care Planning Team. "We will ask the kids, and if they say yes, we can ask them to qualify their yes with how much time they can offer." Furrowing her brow, Jodi expresses one of her real concerns. "But you know my dad will not want to share too many details about his health, and he absolutely will not want to talk about his personal financial information."

"Right." Jackson thinks for a couple of minutes. "So, let's make this as a family project. As CPT members, each participant creates an overview of an option and then discusses it. As a result, we will better understand why a particular option is eliminated or kept for further consideration. We will see how eligibility requirements and the funding of various options play a role in the planning process. You let the kids know that when it comes to a final decision, an advisor or two will be involved to help your parents determine the most feasible option for them. Others can do the same."

"You're right. You're right!" Jodi is ecstatic with relief at Jackson offering a practical arrangement so they can move forward. "OK, Dad will be more comfortable understanding it's a family project. We'll have all three generations participate, with a degree of privacy to keep Dad comfortable."

"And cooperative," Jackson mutters.

As it turns out, both Nicole and Erik want to be included in the CPT. Even if families disagree during the process, it usually does not drive them apart. They often acknowledge the solution is in the best interests of the person they love and will unburden the caregiver. They may feel a bond for helping arrange for the safety and care of their family member."

CHAPTER 11

Figuring Out Today's and Tomorrow's Care Budget

"Your task is not to foresee the future, but to enable it."

— *ANTOINE DE SAINT-EXUPERY*

The Jones family has established their CPT members. Another major element of a care plan is affordability. To be sustainable, the plan must work with the current budget, but also with a future budget. Life events, such as unemployment, births, deaths, divorce, retirement, health issues, etc., all need to be considered.

In order to know what is feasible in terms of a general financial commitment, it is helpful, if not necessary, to get a grasp of the present-day costs for various care facilities and in-home services. Several major insurers and associations offer links to current cost-of-care studies and tools. These sites illustrate how the cost of care varies based on the care setting, geographic location, and level of care required. Although most people recognize the cost for health care continually increases, it is not unusual to experience sticker shock when you see actual and projected costs for extended or long-term care.

What is especially engaging and enlightening about these geographical cost-of-care studies is that you can enter various cost percentage increases (like three percent or four percent) to get estimates of future costs five to thirty years into the future. This tool for estimating future care costs aids in formulating a realistic plan in the present that is also sustainable long term.

This is instructional but also very sobering information. It has the same effect on the Jones family.

> The family is screen-sharing on their Zoom call and reviewing costs by manipulating the cost-of-care study tool. After a lively discussion about the drivers of the cost of care, the Jones family lapses into a pensive silence.
>
> Nicole breaks the silence by sharing a conversation she had with her cousin. "Tyson, who is a first responder, volunteered for extra work shifts during the pandemic. He shared some really heartbreaking stories about the personal effect the shortage of qualified medical and nonmedical workers has had not just on patients but also his buddies and their families. Watching family members look frantic and sick people looking terrified was awful for them. Think of how many families have no plan, no idea of what to do over the long term for someone they care about who survived the ordeal, or simply is no longer comfortable living on their own. You'd think more people would now consider doing some extended and long-term care planning."
>
> Picking up his sister's thread, Erik says, "We all need an affordable, practical plan but let's start with a plan to keep our grandparents safe for the long haul."
>
> Grandpa, happy to become the center of his grandchildren's affection, laughingly teases, "Let's hope Grandma and I are in it for the long haul."
>
> "You have to be," Erik responds, smiling broadly, "since we are all planning for it. And plans work!"

Turning his attention back to the cost of care chart that Jodi still has up on her screen, Erik asks, "What's the difference between a home care aide and home health aide?"

Erik's question is important. Specialized definitions and terminology should be clarified. In most cases, answers can often be found, as in this case, right on the website.

Jodi reads aloud. "A homemaker aid refers to nonclinical help, such as meal prep and companionship, while home health aides, or they may be called patient care assistants, help with daily activities such as cleaning, bathing, toileting, dressing, housekeeping, scheduling, transferring, shopping for groceries, and serving meals. If qualified, some home health aides can check vital signs such as pulse, temperature, and respiration rate."

Definitions are a starting point but the CPT will need to consult a professional. For example, aside from the basic information, when it comes to in-home care, there is a minimum number of hours for which you can hire either type of in-home help. There may be added travel, meals, or other costs as well. There is the issue of deciding if you want to engage an agency that does background checks, certifications, insurance, etc. or take that role on yourself.

Grandma Carolyn won't be in the hospital or recovery facility for long. The family needs to quickly discover a suitable option and build towards a sustainable financial plan. The first phase of Step Three is to get organized by creating a simple summary of facts.

CHAPTER 12

Family Forms A Dynamic Team

"Many Hands Make Work Light; Many Ideas Open the Way"

— *HMONG PROVERB*

For the sake of privacy and efficiency, it is important that only necessary information, relevant to considering various options, be presented in a summary format to the CPT. The Care Guide is a good resource for creating a quick summary from which the CPT can work.

How does the list look for Grandma and Grandpa Jones? Behind the scenes, Jodi worked with her father to put a basic summary together for the next zoom call.

"Hi everyone, thanks for joining. In order to move forward, let me share a summary Grandpa and I put together using family history and information from several of the Care Guide questionnaires and worksheets. Thanks to Nicole for the work she did with Grandpa. This summary will help us as we consider and eliminate various limited, extended, or long-term care options. At the end of the process, it will help Grandpa explain to specialists why certain options appeal to him and Grandma."

Jodi presents the following summary:

- "Grandpa is a veteran.
- Grandpa receives Social Security benefits.
- Grandma receives spousal Social Security benefits.
- Their income is supplemented by a modest amount from savings and investments.
- They are proud they have no mortgage on their home, which has increased in value since they purchased it.
- They both qualify for Medicare and have Medicare Advantage policies.
- Grandpa has a Whole Life Insurance Policy, but as you all know, he has stated unequivocally that beneficiary proceeds are to be equally divided between his grandchildren, Erik and Nicole.
- They drew up a will, but it has not been updated for many years.
- Both of them, thanks to Step One, the Care Guide, now have advanced medical directives, a durable power of attorney for health care or property, and a do-not resuscitate order."

With the summary completed and updated documents, the CPT can move on to long-term care options. It makes for a more relevant exercise when each CPT member's assignment relates to their own potential planning needs. However, the Jones family must make the grandparents their first priority since time is not on their side.

CHAPTER 13

Build a Knowledge Base about Long-Term Care Options

"Happiness is not a goal, it's a by-product."

— ELEANOR ROOSEVELT

Although they feel some pressure to hurry and find a long-term solution for the grandparents, Grandpa is pleased to see other generations benefits from the steps, since, after all, it's a family project!

Evident on this latest Zoom call, caregiver Jodi's tone has gone from overwrought to encouraged to cautiously upbeat. "Hello everyone. I am happy to tell you that we got Grandma and Grandpa's necessary documentation done. We found a local estate planner to update the wills, etc." Looking pleased, she pauses and then proudly announces, "Dad and I realized we also were missing some important documents. We worked with the same firm and created missing documents for ourselves as well! None of you will be asked to make decisions for us without knowing our preferences."

Erik says, "And it reminded my wife and I to update our wills which we should have done after the birth of our daughter. We are not planning any additions to the family, so we hope this will serves us well for a long, long time."

Erik's remark brings on some family teasing about having another child. Grandpa James relaxes as he sees the process is not focused only on him and Grandma.

Erik, laughing along with the CPT, tries to redirect the group. "Mom assigned us different options to look into. Who has long-term care insurance?"

As the CPT investigates different options for the grandparents, they will discover that many long-term care options do not involve insurance. However, traditional or standalone long- term care insurance is often a popular suggestion. If the option seems to fit, they will engage an agent or advisor for a more in-depth review.

Traditional Long-Term Care Insurance

Jodi answers Erik's question about long-term care insurance. "I looked at traditional long-term care insurance. I discovered there are at least three basic issues for Grandpa and Grandma. Let me share my screen so you can see my summary. The first issue is suitability. Is the insurance product appropriate for them, based on their goals and financial situation? The second issue is underwriting. Will they qualify based on their past and current health status? The third issue is affordability and sustainability. Can they pay current and future premiums? Like life insurance, the base price of a long-term care insurance policy is age sensitive. At their ages, and given their past and current health conditions, if my parents were offered a policy, it is not likely to be affordable."

Nicole candidly asks, "So where do we go from here?"

That's a great question, and it's a pretty common one. Sadly, many people are quick to dismiss finding a solution if the first option doesn't fit. In Step Three, you examine multiple options.

Is self-funding a smart option for the grandparents given their growing care needs and advancing age? From information gathered for their Care Guide, we know statistically at least one of the grandparents will live into their eighties or beyond. We also know they have made it very clear they paid off their mortgage so they could age at home. They have no interest in moving, no matter how lovely the facility may be!

Self-Funding Extended or Long-Term Care Expenses

Currently, medical costs are estimated to consume about fifteen percent of an average retiree's annual expenses. If we add a future estimate for long-term care costs, the complications of market timing, liquidity, and the potential for exhausting spousal lifestyle or care funds, self-funding can be a risky proposition.

From the summary, we know the grandparents have been good savers. They also need additional care to begin right away. So, in their case, self-funding does not appear to be a bad option. But a closer look at their financial questionnaire, completed during Step One, reveals a red flag. Like so many of their generation, the grandparents rely heavily on Social Security benefits to supplement their investment and savings income.

Social Security

When Social Security was launched in 1935, you had to be sixty-five years old to qualify for full retirement benefits. Back then, you could say that the actuaries got it right since the average life expectancy was sixty-two years. However, life expectancies have steadily increased, resulting in a financially stressed system. Additional changes to the Social Security program are likely.

Currently, full retirement age is increasing incrementally from sixty-six years to sixty-seven years and is likely to be pushed further out. However, currently a worker may begin receiving Social Security retirement benefits as early as age sixty-two. By claiming before full retirement age, monthly benefits will be permanently reduced by as much as thirty percent.

There are many aspects of the Social Security program that we could cover, but that is beyond the scope of this overview. There are numerous websites, articles, agents, and specialists available for personalized advice.

So, does relying on Social Security income impact the Jones grandparents' self-funding option?

> Grandpa James kicks off the next zoom call. After greetings are exchanged, he shares some information, sending a signal of cooperation to the CPT. "Your mom and I spoke with a Social Security specialist. Since Social Security benefits make up a good portion of our income, we could outlive our current income or be forced to accept government assistance if our resources are depleted too quickly by paying for extended home care."
>
> Grandpa James wants to be clear this situation it isn't about a lack of good budgeting. In his mind, it's just the way the system works. Not wanting to share details of his own income, he offers a general example.
>
> "Let me share the simple example your mom and I saw. Let's say my current Social Security monthly income is $3,000 and Grandma receives $1,500 as my spouse. In this example, Grandma receives a spousal benefit based on my work record. She claimed at her full retirement age, so her benefit is half of my full retirement age benefit of $3,000. But when one spouse passes away, the other one is left with a diminished Social

Security income to cover living expenses plus extended or long-term care expenses."

Quickly shifting the conversation at the mention of her parents passing away, Jodi lightens the mood and encourages the CPT research more on their own. "You each should access the Social Security website at www.ssa.gov/myaccount and create an account. Make sure your personal information and work history is accurately recorded. The site also has a Plan for Retirement section that calculates retirement benefit estimates by:

- Choosing a future age to begin receiving retirement benefits in years and months or you can use the age scroll bar
- Choosing a future date to begin receiving retirement benefits
- Entering the average annual income you expect to earn until retirement."

The CPT enjoys working with the tool and, after a discussion, they conclude that given the prospect of their potential longevity, limited savings, and dependency on dual Social Security income available to cover escalating care costs, self-funding is not a viable option for Grandpa and Grandma.

Grandpa suddenly interjects, reminding everyone he is very much engaged in this planning exercise and has his own financial priorities. "Before we move onto another option, I promised your grandma I would remind everyone that Grandma and I want a plan that doesn't burden Jodi or Jackson—or any of you for that matter—with bills for our care. Jodi and Jackson love spoiling their grandchildren, our great grandchildren. We are so pleased they started a savings fund for them. Funding our care would interrupt, if not end, that heartfelt gesture."

"What kind of savings plan?" Nicole asks, glancing around at the others. "Can I contribute too?"

Resource Allocation Challenges

"We opened a 529 plan for them," Jackson explains to Nicole. "529 plans, legally known as qualified tuition plans, are sponsored by states, state agencies, or educational institutions. The name comes from Section 529 of the Internal Revenue Code. If you start early, as we did, it's an excellent vehicle to fund education costs. We investigated other vehicles, such as money saved in a Roth IRA, a Custodial UGMA, or an UTMA account, which can be used for purposes other than education. We did a comparison, and we decided on a 529 plan. We liked that a 529 plan can be used for graduate school, not just undergraduate school, and depending on state law, may be passed on to the next generation."

"So you can see, Nicole," Grandpa says, nodding a thanks to Jackson, "my concern is that if your parents need to contribute to our care, it could very well interfere not only with funding the 529 plan but also with their retirement plans."

As a result of using the three steps, the Jones family is establishing good avenues of communication. Grandpa, as proud as he is of being independent, realizes self-funding and traditional insurance options will not work for him and his wife. As a result of working with the CPT, without resentment or anger, he reaches that conclusion in sync with his family.

Additionally, the discussion about the 529 plan is a perfect example of how open dialogue leads to more family cohesiveness. While not directly connected to the need for an extended care solution, everyone now understands how the lack of a financially sound extended care plan could negatively influence the success of the 529 plan or his daughter's retirement plan.

It's now time to move on to another option that may work for the grandparents. Hopefully, there will be no more red flags!

CHAPTER 14

What's the Deal with Medicaid and Medicare?

"The important thing is never to stop questioning."

— ALBERT EINSTEIN

The COVID-19 pandemic demonstrated that aging in a care facility is definitely not on everyone's budget or bucket list! With telehealth and wearable health tracking devices becoming more mainstream, some health-care companies are considering the inclusion or expansion of various home health-care benefits in Medicare Advantage programs. States are also reviewing the home health-care benefits available to Medicaid beneficiaries.

Erik, unfamiliar with the ins and outs of government programs, brings up Medicare and Medicaid as possible options. "According to the summary, Grandma and Grandpa both qualify for Medicare and have Medicare Advantage plans."

Jodi responds. "I looked into that option before investigating long-term care insurance. Medicare is an entitlement program, meaning that everyone who reaches age sixty-five and is entitled to receive Social Security benefits also receives Medicare. Medicare covers medically necessary acute care, such as doctor visits, prescription drugs, and hospital stays. Except for specific circumstances, Medicare does not pay for most long-term care services or personal care, such as help with bathing or supervision, which is considered custodial care. Medicare does not provide long-term care coverage or custodial care unless medical care is needed."

Erik continues the query, "But they also have Medicare Advantage coverage. Does that cover long-term care?"

"Medicare Advantage plans generally cover specialized care, such as stays in a skilled nursing facility, hospice, respite care, and eligible home health services," Jodi says. "Some Medicare Advantage plans now cover certain long-term care and at-home care services. However, emphasis is on certain. It doesn't provide the care and services that we need to keep your grandparents at home over the long haul, as you put it. I also looked at Medigap plans. Medigap plans are intended to fill the gaps in Medicare insurance. However, even the most comprehensive of Medigap plans does not cover long-term care needs. These policies currently do not pay for assisted living, Alzheimer's disease, custodial care, personal care, or adult day care."

Erik, hoping to find the right answer, asks, "Maybe they qualify for Medicaid?"

Jodi looks a bit sheepish as she responds. "Your grandparents don't like the idea of the government controlling their care options."

"Medicaid is a welfare program," Grandpa states forcefully to make sure everyone understands how strongly he feels about this option. "Medicaid is a public assistance program that helps pay medical costs for individuals with limited income and assets. To be eligible for Medicaid coverage, you must meet the program's strict income and asset guidelines. We don't qualify, we don't want to qualify, and we don't expect to access a government assistance program. It's for people who haven't been as lucky as us. We don't want to have to spend or give away what we have in order to qualify for government assistance."

He pauses a moment for emphasis. "Also, my friends tell me that the process is complicated and the ongoing paperwork will probably have to be handled with the help of a family member. And worst of all, you lose control over your choices."

Not exactly understanding his grandpa's reaction, Erik thinks back to what their mom shared about how his grandparents' generation was impacted by events very different from what he has experienced.

Grandpa James's response also surprises Nicole. However, one rule of the CPT is to respect different viewpoints. "Got it, Grandpa," she says.

Seeing everyone nodding their heads, it takes Grandpa a moment to absorb the support. A smile starts to cross his face as he looks as each of the people he loves accept his opinion, whether they agree or not.

Erik brings up a topic about which he knows his grandpa is proud. "I saw on the summary that Grandpa is a veteran. Dad, you're also a vet. Can Grandpa use VA benefits for long-term care needs?"

"Both Grandpa and I are veterans, but I suspect we qualify for different levels of benefits. I contacted Dan, a specialist in veteran benefits. I consulted him concerning veteran benefits for both Grandpa and myself. Grandpa and I will do a detailed review with him to determine if Grandpa is entitled to any benefits, what is involved in accessing benefits, and if those benefits can change over time. He has the most exhaustive resource list that you can imagine."

The CPT is glad to finally hear about an option that may be helpful. Jodi wants to build on the positive vibe and continues by mentioning a friend who has parents who also want to age in their home. "My friend told me they secured some funding for long-term care expenses through a reverse mortgage."

There is dead silence. The positive vibe disappears. The reactions are anything but positive.

CHAPTER 15

The Home as a Funding Solution for Aging-in-Place

> "Always desire to learn something useful."
>
> — SOPHOCLES

The Jones family's reaction to the mention of a reverse mortgage is by no means unusual. Historically, largely relegated as a product of last resort for the financially infirm, work done by the Academy for Home Equity in Financial Planning at the University of Illinois Urbana-Champaign elevated the status of reverse mortgage lending. Changes made by the U.S. Department of Housing and Urban Development (HUD) in 2014 to the Home Equity Conversion Mortgage (HECM) further solidified reverse mortgages as a financial planning tool. The home as an asset for retirement income planning and as a funding solution for aging-in-place has increasingly gained acceptance. However, the vast majority of consumers and financial advisors still do not utilize home equity as an effective planning tool.

An expert in the field of reverse mortgages, Harlan Accola from Movement Mortgage shared his experience.

> Many older Americans fear they will outlive their money in retirement or that they won't be able to afford health care. With roughly two-thirds of the average older American's net worth tied up in home equity, the strategic use of home equity, and consequently reverse mortgages, should be a key part of any retirement and health care planning conversation. Older Americans over the age of 62 now own over $12 Trillion dollars in home equity that is doing absolutely nothing. Quite frankly, it is foolish for advisors or homeowners to ignore this huge asset! It should be a part of any sound retirement plan. Recent research indicates that the longer one lives in retirement, the more valuable using a reverse mortgage will be. In fact, using home equity is no different than using a savings account, it is money you have saved to spend in the future when you need it! A reverse mortgage simply turns some of your equity into spendable funds while guaranteeing you may live in your house for as long you wish!"

There is still a lot of misinformation out there about how today's reverse mortgages work. Many individuals fear they will have to give up ownership and the title to the home if they elect this option. The Jones family is no exception.

> Mentioning the potential of a reverse mortgage as a good planning option caused the positive vibe to disappear on the last Zoom call, so Jodi opens the following week's call on a positive note. "Hi! Well, we are certainly learning a good deal as Grandma and Grandpa's Care Planning Team!" However, when Jodi brings up the idea of a reverse mortgage again, Jodi's father immediately becomes alarmed and defensive.

"I am proud to say Grandma and I do not have a mortgage on our home. We do not want to lose the house to a bank or have you owe a bunch of money to repay any sort of mortgage when we are both gone."

Confused, almost tearing up, and looking around for support, Nicole blurts out, "I want to keep my grandparents' house in the family. I have such wonderful memories of holidays and summer at their house."

Erik adds more generational color to the family's attachment. "Every time I say we are going over to Grandma Carolyn's house, my daughter rubs her belly and says, 'Yay! Grandma's house smells good. How many of Grandma's yummy cupcakes can I have?'"

Grandpa looks very touched and says, "I will mention that to Grandma. She will be very pleased!"

Jodi comments, "I understand everyone's reaction. Actually, I initially had the same reaction. But my friend shared with me that now there are reverse mortgages which stipulate that no borrower can ever owe more than the value of the house regardless of how long the occupant lives or what housing values do. The home stands for the debt, not the borrower nor their heirs. This non-recourse feature protects the borrower and their estate from being obligated to provide additional resources to cover the debt when the loan becomes due and payable, and the home is sold. However, we do need to maintain the house and pay the taxes."

Grandpa James puffs up his chest without realizing the gesture isn't visible from the angle of the Zoom window. He states quite firmly, "We are steadfast in those areas!"

"How do they figure out how much money Grandpa can get?" Nicole asks, reminding everyone that the devil is in the details!

"My understanding," says Jodi, "is that you can access a percentage of the home equity as cash, fixed monthly advances, or a line of credit. How much money you can get is based on the current value of the house, the interest rate, and the age of the youngest borrower or non-borrowing spouse if applicable. I invited a specialist to join our call in a couple of minutes. She can offer us advice and answer any questions we may have. Let me admit her."

Moments later, the advisor, Cheryl, joins the Zoom call.

"Hello everyone," she states. "First, let me thank you for inviting me on the call this evening. I have worked in the reverse mortgage field for more than 15 years. I've seen many positive changes, especially important as we discuss James and Carolyn's options with regard to the home they love which houses many treasured family memories."

Jackson responds, "We appreciate you taking the time to meet with us."

Smiling, Cheryl, continues. "Here is how I would like to proceed. I will share some information with you, answer questions, address concerns, and set up a follow-up call. I will begin with an overview of reverse mortgages and, at the conclusion of our time together, I hope we will see that today's reverse mortgages provide qualified homeowner's a good deal of flexibility in terms of funding care needs. Loan officers can discuss using a line of credit or a loan to pay for care services, pay long-term care insurance premium, avoid penalties for early withdrawals from qualified plans, avoid poor market timing if forced to liquidate funds, and so on."

CHAPTER 16

Putting the Plan in Place: Multiple Options Fit the Bill!

"The smallest deed is better than the grandest intention."

— ANONYMOUS

The CPT recognized that government welfare and insurance options were not suitable and/or viable for the grandparents. Instead, the CPT discovered a combination of options that would work. They engaged specialists to examine, in detail, Medicare plan benefits, veteran benefits, and the grandparent's home as a funding source that would allow them to age-in-place.

Jodi is no longer caught in reverse generational responsibilities, where she becomes the parent and her parents become the children. An incredible burden has been lifted. Everyone feels more stable, more hopeful, and more settled with a workable plan in place. The CPT—particularly Grandpa James and Jodi—avoided generational stress, discord, caregiver burnout, and financial hardship by engaging at various levels and at various times in my three steps. They created a tailored generational family plan. The exercise left Jodi wondering if there were additional options available for her if she also lives a long life and eventually needs care like her parents.

Like the Jones family, your family should personalize the three steps to start the conversation, understand family dynamics, become educated, and engage with professionals to secure a plan. The three steps lead families to a healthier, more financially secure, and peaceful place.

SECTION III

A Caregiver's Lessons Learned

CHAPTER 17

The Sandwich Generation Issue Solved—Or is it?

> "What do we live for, if not to make life less difficult for each other?"
>
> — *GEORGE ELIOT*

The Jones family achieved a level of harmony while working together as a team, which initially started out as a recognition that Jodi's life was slowly being consumed by caregiving.

As we saw with the Jones family, becoming caught in the sandwich generation typically starts with just helping with a chore here or there. Gradually, caregiver responsibilities increase along with care needs. Until it became evident that Jodi was becoming overwhelmed, other family members and friends, although aware, did not feel comfortable or know how to acknowledge the impact it was having on Jodi and her parents. Jodi's story is typical. Brothers and sisters and other family members do not always share equally in the care of parents. I have friends who share this book to introduce the subject and engage in a discussion about how the steps can help the family work towards a solution.

Let's check back in to see how the Jones family is doing now that Jodi and Jackson, while still part of the sandwich generation, are no longer experiencing the many negative and unwanted challenges brought about by the absence of a plan for the grandparents' well-being.

Jodi looks and feels much better now her parents are secure. They are on board with the plan, can afford it, and importantly, it allows them to age at home. Jackson is happy his wife can enjoy a more normal work/life balance and has time to do some fun things with him and their grandchildren. Jodi arranges a CPT wrap-up call, minus her dad, to remind everyone they will periodically review Grandpa and Grandma's plan.

Despite her father's reluctance and sometimes forceful remarks, utilizing the three steps pulled this family together instead of apart. But she will not soon forget how unaware she was of the effect her caregiver duties was having on other generations.

Jodi is motivated to pay it forward. "Hey, honey, take a look at this."

Jackson leans over and looks at Jodi's iPad. "What am I seeing?"

"Look at this chart. It illustrates findings from the National Alliance for Caregiving (NAC) and AARP's research report, Caregiving in the U.S. 2020. The new study finds that the number of family caregivers in the US increased by 9.5 million from 2015 to 2020 to total fifty-three million people and encompasses more than one in five Americans. Caregiving in the U.S. 2020 also reveals that family caregivers are in worse health compared to five years ago."

Gently, Jackson reminds Jodi, "Now you know why we are all so glad that we did the three steps. You were definitely in that statistic. It probably has increased quite a bit since 2020."

"Erik is a Gen Xer and Nicole is a Millennial. They are adults!"

"Right." Not sure where the conversation is headed, he adds a qualifier to acknowledge his agreement, "They are busy adults!"

Puzzled that Jackson isn't making the connection, Jodi clarifies by saying, "My point is, as we age, like our parents, we may need help. We saw how the amount we need to save for health care related expenses is substantial and growing. What if one of us must be the caregiver for the other? We know first-hand what caregiving does to the health and finances of the caregiver. What if we cannot handle each other's needs? That means our children will get caught in the sandwich generation and become caregivers. We should look at what planning options are out there for us. I suggest a redo."

"A redo?"

"Of the three steps. We are in pretty good health, we are financially making good progress with our investments and savings, the kids are busy with their lives, and we are aware that extended health-care resources are not abundant. Why risk blowing up everyone's lifestyle, career paths, and retirement resources if we can plan and take that risk off the table?"

Nodding, Jackson replies, "Let me set up a call to run this by the kids."

Now that people can get together in person again since COVID restrictions have eased, Jackson, Jodi, and Nicole meet at Erik's new home. Once they get the children settled for naps, Jackson starts the talk.

"First, I want to compliment both of you for how well you handled yourselves as part of your grandparents' Care Planning Team. They are adjusting to having help for Grandma, and you know Grandpa, he is controlling every detail of her care." Jackson pauses. His children brush off the compliment but smiling faces say otherwise.

Jodi puts her hand on Jackson's arm. "Now it's our turn."

Smiles disappear. Panic engulfs Erik's and Nicole's faces. "What!" they almost shout in unison. They think they are about to hear one of their parents has been diagnosed with something requiring extended care or worse.

Jodi continues, "Oh dear, I see I need to explain. One of our biggest concerns is that the obligation to provide extended or long-term care for us could interfere with your career path, your health, your lifestyle, and your retirement." She can almost see behind their expressions that they are thinking about the promotion she passed up and the deteriorating effect caregiving had on her health. "Let me remind you that as we discovered workable options by using the three steps, the entire family, including your grandparents, started to look more relaxed and confident. We want to do the same for the next generation—you!"

Erik responds, "But isn't this too early? There isn't anything wrong, right?" He looks to his sister for backup.

Nicole takes over. "Is there something we don't know? I agree with Erik. Grandma and Grandpa are older. I'm so glad we found a couple of options that worked so they can age at home. But you guys are, well, younger."

Jodi answers, "As I recall, you both were concerned about the effect of providing care for your grandparents was having on me, and that was before they ended up at the hospital. Erik, your job required you to move further away. What if either of your next job or promotion moves you even farther away? It is expensive to fly back and forth and not very practical."

Understandably, it is hard for Erik and Nicole to imagine their parents in need of extended or long-term care. So many pictures and activities on social media and advertising are geared toward joyful, youthful retirement images. But that hasn't stopped the hands of time or events like the pandemic. Becoming a caregiver is not confined to just eldercare needs. Erik and Nicole gave Jackson a brochure to help Jodi realize she and others were being negatively impacted by her caregiver duties. To refocus the discussion, Jodi shares a chart about the impact caregiving can have on caregiver income, finances, and retirement plans.

Jodi never indicated that caring for her parents had a financial impact on her retirement plans, although everyone suspected it went beyond the lost wages from passing on the promotion.

According to an AARP Family Caregiving Cost survey, most family caregivers incur steep out-of-pocket costs related to caregiving. Long-distance caregivers, defined as family caregivers living more than one hour from the care recipient, incurred the highest out-of-pocket costs; however, even caregivers living with their care recipient incurred high costs.

It might mean working different hours, fewer or more hours, and taking paid or unpaid time off.

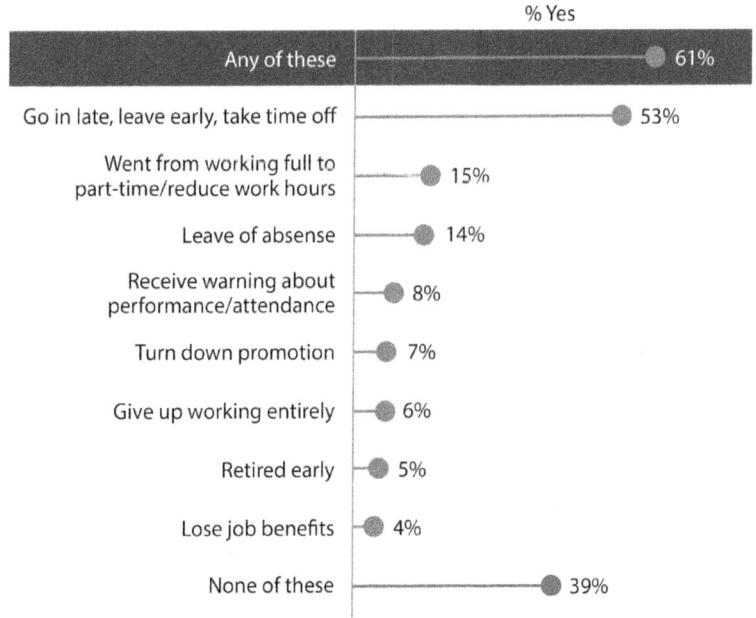

Impact on Caregivers Finances, Work, and Lifestyle

% Yes

Any of these	61%
Go in late, leave early, take time off	53%
Went from working full to part-time/reduce work hours	15%
Leave of absense	14%
Receive warning about performance/attendance	8%
Turn down promotion	7%
Give up working entirely	6%
Retired early	5%
Lose job benefits	4%
None of these	39%

"Caregiving in the US," Pew Research Center, Washington D.C. May 2020, Figure 69, accessed 12/05/2020
https://www.aarp.org/content/dam/aarp/ppi/2020/05/full-reort-caregiving-in-the-united-states.doi.10.26419-2F
ppi.00103.001.pdf

And then there is the effect on your own family if you need to cut back on other spending, which can undermine a family's future financial security. Caregivers may have to reduce contributions to their own retirement savings which can result in a long-term impact on savings and Social Security benefits.

> Jodi continues to state her case to her children. "Sixty-two percent of caregivers who participated in the AgingCare.com survey say the cost of caring for a parent has impacted their ability to plan for their own financial future. Why would we risk doing that to you when we have other options?"
> Nicole, looking pensive, tries to wrap her head around why her parents are sharing this research. "So, what you're saying is that the age of a family member isn't the decisive factor but rather the serious consequences of not planning that you want to avoid, for all of us? So, what exactly are you suggesting?"
> "Dad and I want to redo the three steps."
> Erik, not aware of the potentially numerous available options, teases, "So, you and Dad intend to pay off your mortgage or maybe use Dad's veteran benefits?"
> Jodi fakes an admonishing glance. "Since Dad and I are younger than your grandparents and in relatively good health, there are many other options for us to consider. We know you would not hesitate to disrupt your lives and your careers to be our caregivers. And maybe you don't want to picture us seriously incapacitated due to an accident or illness, or aging into the same stage of care needs as your grandparents, but that just isn't smart."
> Jackson, characteristically, is more forceful in his approach. "We saw what caregiving did to Mom, and how it stressed all of us. We simply do not want that for you. Here's what we will do. Let's arrange a series of Zoom calls since that worked pretty well before. Meanwhile, Mom and I will complete Step One and let you know our plans for Step Two."

Nicole looks hesitant. "OK, how many options are there? Maybe we could Zoom a little less frequently than we did with Grandma and Grandpa? We aren't as pressed, and I am still struggling to see you needing care. Plus, I want to leave time in case I want to do additional research after we talk through potential options."

Playfully, Erik says, "Yup, looks like more details to investigate. Right up your alley, sis."

Nicole thoughtfully responds, "Right! But I can always get my advisor to help out. She is well connected to specialists!"

Even after experiencing the demands and hardships associated with the absence of an extended and long-term care plan, it's not uncommon to just put off planning for oneself or other family members. However, planning is a multi-step process and the Jones family has already learned a good deal. Moving forward, flexibility and availability may involve a change in the makeup of the CPT.

CHAPTER 18

Retirement Planning is More Than a Simple Math Problem

> "Do, What you are going to do in longevity. Not just what happens tomorrow."
>
> — SKITCH HENDERSON

Erik and Nicole's reaction to planning for their parents is typical of their generation. It's a real struggle for younger generations to understand the positive role early long-term care planning plays in securing an envisioned lifestyle and retirement. But generations are living longer and longevity brings with it both the good and the less-than-good.

Many people remember their grandparents who seemed able to pay for their own care. Memories are not always a reliable resource. People are living longer and one source of retirement income has seen major changes in the last decade. The world of pension plans has dramatically changed over the years, moving away from defined benefit plans which provided retirees a specified payment to defined contribution plans. Defined contribution plans are saving plans that allows both employers (if they choose) and employees (if they chose) to contribute. Specific payments to retirees are not promised. Familiar examples of contribution plan are 401(k) plans, 403(b) plans, and simplified employee pension (SEP) plans. These plans, properly funded and invested, play an important role in retirement budgeting. Fortunately, both Jackson and Jodi have plans that will help secure their retirement unless they have to prematurely dig into the funds for unplanned extended and long-term care expenses.

Another traditional resource was Social Security benefits. As we saw with the grandparents, when figuring Social Security benefits into your overall retirement financial picture, the trick is to understand some of the basic yet complex rules. And it is tricky! Best to start with a simple grasp of foundational information. Like the Jones family, you can get a general sense of it by visiting the Social Security online services website. However, changes are expected so check back for updates or consult with a specialist to help you personalize and understand the current and projected impact of various benefit elections.

> Lacking the immediate pressure they felt in finding a sustainable solution for the grandparent's care needs and noting his children's lack of enthusiasm for a redo, Jackson changes gears. He suspects that having fun while learning something that relates to their own lives will reinvigorate Erik and Nicole's interest. Uncovering their own projected longevity may do the trick. They will use the Social Security online calculator to estimate the average number of additional years a person can expect to live, based only on the gender and date of birth entered. He thought it may also surprise them to learn how many years they will need funds to support their retirement after leaving the workforce.

Jackson kicks off the next Zoom call by saying, "Let's have some fun! I shared a link in the chat box for a site that allows us a peek at our expected longevity."

Nicole and Erik whip out their phones and start to play with the calculator.

After everyone announces their projected longevity and has sufficiently teased one another, Jackson gets their attention. "I'm glad you guys are enjoying this exercise. If you recall, while doing the three steps with your grandparents, we saw the impact of potential health-care costs on what your grandparents thought was a solid retirement income plan. You both have friends whose baby boomer parents or relatives have health issues or are experiencing the effects of aging."

"True, we can relate," Nicole says, including Erik in her response. "Our grandparents always seemed pretty healthy, but as they grew older, they needed more and more help. Since it was gradual, we sort of ignored it. Then, we couldn't help but notice Mom's health change and Grandma's frailty. Then everything got seriously jammed."

This little exercise was fun and made all of them think more realistically about the demands longevity can place on retirement planning. Health care costs must figure into the planning and gradual but increasing extended care needs and costs also need to be added to the equation.

Jodi and Jackson are in the prime earning years of their careers and are currently saving for retirement. But how many of us think about who is subsidizing our health-care costs? Currently, they participate in an employer-sponsored health-care plan. Costs are deducted directly out of their paycheck. It's easy to forget that during retirement, health-care costs are paid by individuals. Those are costs over which you have little control. If chronic or serious long-term health issues arise, unplanned costs may seriously impact retirement finances. Or what if you are young but surprised by an unplanned health event? Unfortunately, thirty-seven percent of long-term care recipients are under sixty-five years old.

In the Zoom call with their children, Jackson relates how the longevity estimates could impact Jodi and his retirement. "As we saw on the site, Mom's life expectancy means she will likely live a long time after she retires. If you think about it, you can control a certain amount of expenses in retirement, like housing costs, travel expenses, clothing, gifts, eating out, and technology related expenditures. We will not have as much flexibility or control over health-care costs, such as Medicare or Medigap premiums, supplemental health insurance premiums, vision or hearing, deductibles, co-pays, prescriptions, over-the-counter medicines, medical equipment, and support services and the wild card, extended or long-term care expenses."

"I think you now understand why a redo of the three steps for us is, well, simply smart," says Jodi. "Financial preparedness for living longer is more than a simple math problem. Here's how we will move forward. We will review with our advisor the potential impact of longevity on our retirement, especially on my side. We will carefully review how and when we figure in Social Security benefits, our pension funds, and various investments, housing, and cost-of-care estimates. Neither one of us wants to cause the other an unduly limited lifestyle by depleting our resources due to extended or long-term care needs. As you know, Jackson and I have completed Step One. We each created our own Care Guide. Next, we will lay out our Care Squad and get back to you. Love you," she says and finishes the call.

The key to avoid exhausting even the largest emergency funds is to plan in advance. The biggest advantage of advance planning is that it opens up a pretty robust list of possible options.

CHAPTER 19

Step Two: Who is Available in Person or Virtually to Lend a Hand?

> "It is not the load that breaks you down.
> It's the way you carry it."
>
> — LENA HORNE

Now that everyone appreciates longevity, individual health care costs, and potential extended care needs can impact retirement plans, Jodi and Jackson move their plan forward by considering the make-up of their Care Squad. In the case of Jodi's parents, distance and availability of their caregiver was not a big issue. But that's not always the case.

We are getting to know the Jones family pretty well, so let's see how they handle it.

After dinner, Jodi and Jackson, glass of wine in hand, move to the living room. Jackson doesn't turn the TV on.

"What's up? You look as if you have something to tell me," says Jodi.

"It's about forming the Care Squad. We probably should not have each other as the only primary person since we may be together. We still need to list Erik and Nicole, but maybe we just give them a sealed copy so they don't have to go to the house before going to the hospital or care facility."

"Good idea."

"I'll let them know."

After talking on the phone with Nicole, he turns back to Jodi. Looking as if he has been admonished, he tells Jodi, "Well, Nicole thought having a sealed copy made good sense, provided we remember to update it. As if!"

Jodi stifles a giggle at Jackson's overreaction.

Jackson then calls Erik, hangs up, and looks at his wife.

"Now what?" Jodi notices Jackson has a curious look on his face.

"Erik wants to have us put a copy in a sealed online vault," Jackson explains. "His friend is familiar with a company that does just that. He said to visit www.getprismm.com and he will have his friend explain the security, access, and convenience to us. He also has a friend that has an app, www.getcarefull.com to help adult children and parents protect their financial resources, savings, credit identity, passwords, and documents. We might want to consider it for your parents. Erik said we should not be afraid to use technology. It does sound interesting."

Technology advances provide, and will continue to provide, a boost to each of the three steps. Younger generations will look to available technologies to monitor parent's care, increase personal involvement, electronically store documents, safely share information, and reduce reliance on face-to-face meetings or care, to name just a few.

CHAPTER 20

Expanding Beyond Family

> "A real friend is one who walks in when the rest of the world walks out."
>
> — WALTER WINCHELL

Although forming a Care Squad is a simple step, it must be practical and efficient. For the CPT to be effective, it's much the same. All members must understand the basic objectives and rules. It isn't unusual to have more than just family members participate, but it should be clearly communicated why the Care Squad or CPT is expanding beyond the family. Nonfamily members need to understand their role, the purpose, process, and promise of the CPT as well.

Jackson is lingering in the kitchen as Jodi makes coffee. Jodi senses that there is something on his mind. She waits. Jackson seems hesitant.

"Let me guess. You want to have Doug as part of the Care Squad," she says.

Jackson is stunned for a moment and then laughs. "Ah, well, yeah, I do."

"It's a great idea! Doug's over here a lot. He already has a spare key in case we lock ourselves out. Besides, Doug is the kind of friend that has become part of the family, if not by blood, then by his good heart, good sense, and loyalty."

Jackson invites Doug, his lifelong best friend, to join him for coffee. Their wives and children are friends and they have vacationed together for years. They sit in the kitchen while Jackson describes how helpful the Care Squad was during the ordeal of Jodi's parent's emergency. They move into the living room and are joined by Jodi.

Doug says, "I am happy to be part of the Care Squad. Thanks for asking me."

Jackson announces he will bring Doug up to speed on the Care Guide and his role as a primary responder for their Care Squad. Doug is flattered to be part of the Care Squad, but Jodi and Jackson want to take his involvement a step further.

"There is a third step in this planning process. Step Three focuses on appropriate options to offset the risk of extended and long-term care. We would like you to be part of our Care Planning Team," Jackson states.

Doug, already impressed with the usefulness of Step One and the simplicity of Step Two, is curious about Step Three and asks about it.

"Basically," Jackson continues, "Step Three is an education process. It's the discovery step. We take turns offering an overview of various options. It will arm us with smart questions to ask a professional once we narrow down options we think work for us."

"I'm in!" Doug's face shows he is both curious and pleased.

To work effectively together, clear and open communication channels are essential. Your CPT may span several generations, making tolerance and recognition of generational orientations critical components.

Jackson, Jodi, and Doug are part of the baby boomer generation, born between 1946 and 1964. As a generation, they tend to be more optimistic than their parents due to the economic boom from postwar reconstruction and the following years of steady industrial development.

Understanding members of the CPT in terms of their personal and lifestyle influencers can involve research or simply sharing memories. Let's continue as Jackson and Doug stroll down memory lane.

"Do you remember the hippie movement during the late sixties?" Doug asks.

Jackson takes a swig of his beer. Looking nostalgic, he replies, "Yes, so many of our boomer friends were free-spirited, open, and interested in social causes. We saw the civil rights, anti-war, and women's movements emerge, and politics become a mass event where I think two more or less defined sides—liberalism and conservativism—became more evident."

Doug continues, "The kids think we are relics when it comes to technology, but we were the first ones to witness the rapid development of technology, accept and appreciate it. I remember when the terms space race became popular. Now technological progress has led to a renewed interest in space activities and a new global space race involving a multitude of public and private entities."

"Plus," Jackson adds, "we lived through the Green Revolution in agriculture and the invention of the television."

Faking a look of disapproval, Doug chimes in, "Which the kids consider old school. They now watch their programs on their phones!"

Undeterred, Jackson presses on. "And don't forget the great advances in medicine. Remember how crazy and almost scary it was when they did the first heart transplant? Nowadays, they transplant all sorts of, of—"

Jodi enters the room and interjects, chuckling, "Parts!"

They share a laugh and dip into the snacks Jodi puts down on the table for them. Before saying goodnight, Doug tells Jackson and Jodi that he is really glad to be part of planning for their future wellbeing as he hopes to be part of it. Jackson says, "Same back at you!"

The friends enjoyed their shared memories, but Jackson, Jodi, and Doug will have to keep in mind that their children come with very different life experiences and are adults. Erik and Nicole were willing to take a back seat while participating in planning for their grandparents, but when it comes to their own parents, it's closer to home. It can be a different story.

Erik is part of Generation X, born between 1965 and 1980. Growing up during the final years of the Vietnam War, Watergate, and the Reagan and Bush Senior era, Gen Xers witnessed the end of the Cold War, the expansion of globalism, the introduction of early home computers, radical changes to the media industry, and the early days of MTV. They grew up with continual change and the introduction of new technologies. Thus, they are accustomed to a changing environment.

Nicole is a member of the Millennial Generation, born between 1981 and 1996. This generation grew up with continual enhancements of technology. They are comfortable accessing online retail and sharing all sorts of opinions and information. They exhibit a discernable preference for experience over product. They research before they commit. They have brought racial and ethnic diversity to the forefront of American society. And Millennial women, like Generation X women, are more likely to participate in the nation's workforce than prior generations.

As the mother of both a Gen Xer who came into the workforce on the cusp of cell phones, the Internet, and social media, and the mother of a Millennial, who grew up when these things were a regular part of daily life, Jodi is aware her children's approach to using the three steps may vary from hers. She is concerned Jackson will not appreciate the children were generationally distanced from planning for their grandparents, but this time it will be different.

A week later, back at the Jones house, the doorbell rings. Jackson ushers Doug in and hands him a cold beer and says, "Thanks for coming." Turning toward the kitchen, he shouts, "Honey, Doug is here, so let's get started."

Jodi is glad to see Doug and really pleased to have him as a member of the CPT. Doug will be less sensitive about certain issues than her husband (and maybe herself as well). She gets the meeting going by explaining where they are at. "We have completed Step One, and you now know where we keep our Care Guides. You have our completed Step Two Care Squad chart. Now onto Step Three."

Jackson takes over, evidently expecting to take the lead. "I explained to Doug," he says, "that our goal is to effectively reduce a bunch of potential negative consequences. 'Plan for the unplanned' is the way I put it. I already discussed how effective it was to have multiple generations on board for when, what we thought might eventually happen with your parents, did!"

"Yes, it could have been a real nightmare, but we all handled it amazingly well." Jodi nods.

Jackson's tone softens as he describes how having a plan for Jodi's parents also avoided continuing interference with Jodi's work/life balance and their contributions to 401k plans, investments, and the 529 Plans they set up for funding their grandchildren's education.

Clearly impressed with how much they have thought this through, Doug still wants some reassurance on his role in the plan. "You're sure the kids are OK with me being part of this?" he asks.

"Oh yeah, Erik told me you probably remember my personal and family history better than I do!"

The look exchanged between Jodi and Doug says there is probably some truth to that statement.

Just then, the doorbell rings again. It's Erik. Jackson ushers him in and goes to the kitchen to get him a cold one.

HOW NOT TO PULL YOUR FAMILY APART

Erik sits down. Once Jackson returns with Erik's beer, he announces Doug will be part of both the Care Squad and the CPT. Erik's unexplained look of relief soon turns into a look of discomfort. After a moment of heavy silence, he confides he will have trouble participating in the CPT. Between his work, his new home, his kids, and obligations with his wife's family, he is feeling pretty pressed. Supportive of his honesty, his parents encourage him to join in whenever he can.

Unfortunately, that sort of support and understanding about planning or providing long-term care is not always the case. If you recall the personal story about the family that I married into, my husband was appointed to the lead position concerning his mother's care. Feeling excluded from responsibility, his brother was jealous, resentful, and uncooperative. We won't even discuss how that weighed on their mother. Too bad we didn't use at least one of the steps to help ameliorate the situation. The silver lining is that the really difficult experience contributed to me developing the three steps.

In other cases, there is an alpha child who feels they must control all aspects of a parent's or sibling's care. It can leave spouses, uncles, aunts, sisters, and brothers feeling resentful and excluded. A friend of mine decided the best solution was to share the three steps with her sister and accept assignments rather than being left out completely.

The Jones family will kick off their CPT meetings with Erik's limited participation. Jodi volunteers to take notes and distribute them to everyone, including Erik. Sharing keeps everyone included and, when working with a larger CPT or spreading the meeting over a longer period, it is helpful to send a summary of each call. It also keeps everyone on the same page and serves as a reminder of the progress being made. In the future, if emotions run high, it will help to remind everyone how and why decisions were made.

CHAPTER 21

Envisioning Your Future Self Through Self-Profiling

"The best gift you can give yourself is the gift of possibility."

— PAUL NEWMAN

The nicest thing about the future is that it starts tomorrow. One of the hardest things about the future is imagining what it will bring. In the case of extended or long-term care planning, most of us know a story about someone's experience with long-term care. A helpful technique in envisioning future care is to imagine a successful extended care plan. From that point, think through all the reasons it would be successful. Then, imagine that the same strategy has underperformed, and think through all the reasons it wouldn't achieve success.

Jackson and Jodi were struggling with envisioning their individual future selves. They found answering this list of questions helpful, enlightening, and fun!

- Do you have a retirement date in mind?
- If applicable, do you think your spouse/partner has the same date in mind?
- Will you want to travel? Do you have a budget in mind for travel and excursions?
- Will you want to entertain? Do you have a location and budget in mind?
- Do you expect to do volunteer work?
- How do you envision your health progressing during the aging process? Anything in particular that could curtail activities?
- Do you expect to remain in your current home and age in place, or downsize, or change location?
- Do you expect to live independently if your spouse/partner/companion predeceases you?
- Do you feel you can fund the lifestyle you envision?
- Do you feel you can fund limited, extended, or long-term care if needed?
- Do you worry about becoming a burden to others as you age?
- Have you completed the necessary documents and medical directives so others know your wishes?
- Do you want to leave a legacy behind? What does that entail?
- Do you know a story about someone who needed extended or long-term care? What would you modify if you were the one needing care? What would you modify if you were the caregiver?

"I wish I had been a fly on the wall," Doug jokes. "Did you two do serious battle?"

"There is no denying that at times it got, shall we say, a bit informative. But it's what you don't know that you don't know that can trip you up," Jackson offers.

"Or what you think you know that you don't know," Doug observes.

Smiling, Jodi adds, "As the artist Francis Picabia said, 'Our heads are round so thoughts can change direction.'"

"Clever!" Jackson smiles and then hesitantly admits, "but seriously, at the end of the day, or the end of multiple dinners, we had a much better idea of why people turn to advisors for help."

"You mean as a referee?" Doug asks.

Jackson replies, "I guess! But more as an interpreter to help us see possibilities."

Although Jodi and Jackson envisioned some things differently, they each heard responses to questions that helped broaden their perspectives. To further boil it down to what is essential, each person should write down five or six keywords to describe how they envision a future care plan to conclude the exercise. It is important to remember it is not about a process, not about a product, not yet about a plan, it's about you.

As a result of the exercise, on the next CPT call, Jodi shares the chart that she and Jackson put together. "This is a quick summary of what we have gathered from documentation, planning exercises, and conversations."

As the CPT reviews the chart, Jodi offers clarifications.

- "Jackson and I have a mortgage on our home which we are not planning to pay off.
- We usually rent that lake cottage near Jackson's parents during our vacation and attend Jackson's annual family reunion. Jackson's parents would like us to live

close to them. We love the area and might consider retiring there since it's familiar and affordable. It isn't too far from here so we could still see our friends.
- In the story of a successful plan that we used to envision our future selves, we discussed our friends who moved into an assisted living facility and seem quite satisfied with the arrangement. I am willing to consider moving into an assisted living facility or continuing care retirement facility but only if it provides a continuum for more extensive care in case one or both of us experience serious health or longevity issues. Of course, that would also depend on my parent's situation.
- We both participate in 401K qualified savings plans. Both employers offer contributions for participants.
- We sometimes carry a small running debt on our credit cards.
- We access health-care coverage through Jackson's employment. Since it's a high deductible health plan, we qualify and contribute to individual health savings accounts.
- We both have employer group disability insurance. Jackson has an additional disability insurance policy that he carries due to our home mortgage.
- I envision retiring before Jackson, who wants to collect the optimal amount of Social Security benefits for which he can qualify since currently there is a financial bonus for delaying his benefit election."

Nicole and Erik simultaneously ask, "What kind of financial bonus?"

Jackson shares with the group that he accessed his Social Security statement at the website *my* Social Security so he could understand the effect of Jodi claiming benefits early and his delay. He also accessed links to nine online supplemental fact sheets. Additionally, Jackson concludes, "It appears it would be wise to include Social Security benefits in our plan, accounting for the timing differences between our plans for claiming benefits, and potential changes to the Social Security program."

Nicole picks up the conversation, and turning to Doug, she adds, "During our grandparent's planning session, we saw the potentially serious financial impact of relying on Social Security income if one of a couple predeceases the other."

Doug responds, as if on cue, "Funny you mention that, Nicole. My oldest sister is living with her husband in a Continuing Care Retirement Community, CCRC for short. The family continually teases her about taking such good care of him. Aside from the fact they have been together for a very long time, the truth is she worries that either of them may not afford the cost of living in the CCRC if his or her Social Security income or pension income is reduced or eliminated. The CCRC maintenance costs are adjusted for inflation each year. She doesn't feel she has much wiggle room. We all tease her about keeping him alive!"

"Thanks Doug," Jackson says looking thoughtful. "We will have to investigate the significant differences between CCRCs and Assisted Living Facilities."

Jodi continues with the summary:

- "Jackson has a whole life insurance policy that he bought years ago. Jackson qualifies for his employer's group life policy for two times his salary.
- I have a term life insurance policy but coverage will soon end unless I convert it. I don't have additional life insurance coverage through my workplace.
- We have a joint investment account from which we recently withdrew a small amount in order to help

Erik and his wife pay bills for a complicated health issue their son experienced.
- Jackson is a very proud veteran. He and Doug served together.
- During Step One, we completed health and property directives, DNA paperwork, etc. We also created a living will."

The question of where you will live in retirement should not be overlooked in the planning process. The grandparents planned to age in their home. They had accessed some of the value of their home via a Reverse Mortgage allowing them to remain at home as they access services. However, Jodi and Jackson are considering alternate living arrangements.

CHAPTER 22

Moving Your Extended or Long-Term Care Plan Forward

> "The most difficult thing is the decision to act, the rest is merely tenacity."
>
> — AMELIA EARHART

At the next meeting, the Care Planning Team shares stories, envisions future plans, and employs longevity and cost of care tools while reviewing Jodi and Jackson's summary. Let's see what else moves the decision-making process along.

Jodi kicks off the next meeting. Erik is not attending so they gather in Jodi and Jackson's living room. "Hi, everyone, one of the great side effects of being a part of the CPT is that we all get together regularly. I think we are all benefiting from this learning/discovery process. Dad had us play around with projecting our longevity. Now, let's play a guessing game that relates to possible retirement locations and their associated care costs. Who would like to guess how many counties there are in the United States?"

Each CPT member throws out a number.

"Doug guessed 2,850, and that was the closest," Jodi concludes when they give their answers. "Currently, there are 3,006 counties in the United States alongside 142 county-equivalents, like boroughs in Alaska and parishes in Louisiana. The point is that costs and local services may vary from one area to another."

"What's my prize?" Doug asks.

"You don't wind up receiving care at a location that isn't your first choice or unaffordable!" Jackson jokes with a dose of reality mixed in.

Doug laughs. "Good point! By taking the current monthly cost and then using one of the insurance geographical cost-of-care calculators to push costs out twenty-five years, I can estimate how much money I would have to save to cover costs in various settings and locations."

Nicole and Doug do some quick math.

"Wow! That's quite a sum!" Doug looks shocked.

Nicole adds, "And let's not forget that the aging Baby Boomer population is estimated to be about seventy-two million people. It's impossible to know where costs will go, other than up! Let's just confidently conclude that it is likely to be a significant number."

"Even if I gave up my favorite restaurant, wine, and poker games," Jackson says, grinning at Jodi, "I don't see us saving that kind of money!"

Jodi smiles, then adds, "Or keeping that amount of money in an emergency fund earning next to nothing! The bottom line is Dad and I don't want to be obligated to keep that amount of money in a low-risk investment, designated only as an emergency extended or long-term care fund. Insurance is a way to leverage our money against funding those ever-increasing costs.

More importantly, we want to do it while we still qualify for various options."

Doug is starting to see the reason his friends want to plan now. "Even with a good financial plan in place, I guess someone who doesn't plan for possible expenses may be obligated to withdraw savings, cash in stocks, or liquidate assets regardless of good or bad market timing. I wonder what our tax advisor would say."

Jackson, who uses the same tax advisor as Doug, remarks, "Nothing that I would want to hear!"

Having your savings and accumulated assets blow up probably wouldn't make for a pretty tax picture. It leaves you vulnerable and dependent on family and friends, or government, state, and/or community services. Expecting help from outside resources comes with emotional complications for both the giver and the receiver. It can mean that someone else or an entity may control your care. That's an unsettling prospect.

Looking into funding vehicles early in your career while there is ample time to accumulate funds is smart. Someone with a High Deductible Health Plan can contribute funds to a Health Savings Account (HSA). An HSA is specifically designed to help pay for medical care costs and, under certain circumstances, long term-care insurance premiums. According to their personal summary, Jodi and Jackson both have HSA accounts.

SECTION IV

Funding Options To Support Financial Stability

CHAPTER 23

A Health Savings Account as a Funding Mechanism

"It's easy to make good decisions when there are no bad options."

— *ROBERT HALF*

A health savings (HSA) account is a tax-advantaged medical savings account that allows account holders to save money for the payment of health-care costs for themselves and their families. The money you contribute to your HSA goes in, grows, and comes out income-tax free when used for qualified medical expenses. HSA funds roll over from year to year with no use-it-or-lose-it limits.

HSAs are not only tax-advantaged savings accounts, but individual account holders may invest the funds. As part of your protection plan, they may help avoid depleting a comprehensive retirement package by providing assistance with long-term care insurance premiums and medical expenses.

At the end of the previous meeting, the group decided to review this funding mechanism which is steadily gaining in popularity. Jodi starts the discussion. "Did you know you can use an HSA account as a long-term care funding mechanism?"

Everyone shakes their head.

Doug doesn't want to upstage Jodi, so he waits to pitch in. "Don't feel bad. Dad and I also thought you couldn't use an HSA account to pay long-term care premiums, and we actually have HSAs!"

Nicole, looking hopeful, mentions, "I know Erik has a flexible savings account at work? Is that the same?"

"No, sorry dear, it isn't," Jodi says, "but I am glad you asked. It's easy to mix the two up since both FSAs and HSAs are pretax accounts you can use to pay for health-care related expenses."

Having piqued everyone's interest, Jodi throws out a second question. "How would anyone who is not contributing to an FSA account open an HSA account?"

"You better just tell us, Mom," says Nicole.

"Actually, there are two ways to open an HSA account," Jodi explains. "Since the HSA belongs to the individual and not the employer, as long as you are covered by a high deductible health plan, you may open and contribute to an HSA. The other way is how Dad and I did it. Since we have a qualifying high deduction health plan through work, we were also able to open an HSA through our employer."

Nicole continues her inquiry. "What if my employer doesn't offer an HSA account? Where can I open one on my own?"

Jodi answers, "First, remember that you cannot contribute to both an HSA and FSA. From what I read, Nicole, you may want to check first with your human resources department since my employer, like others, contributes money to my HSA. I suspect my employer may pick up the fees as well. I found this helpful chart to explain the triple tax advantages of HSAs.

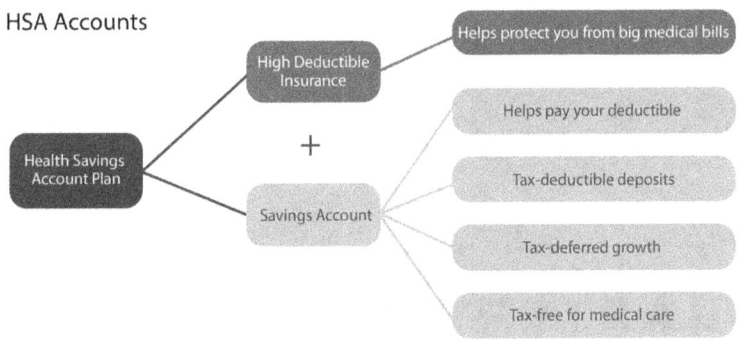

Because the administration of an HSA is a taxpayer responsibility, advisors and consumers are strongly encouraged to consult a tax advisor before opening an HSA. Information is available from the Internal Revenue Service (IRS) for taxpayers, which can be found online at the IRS website at IRS.gov IRS Publication 969, Health Savings Accounts and Other Tax-Favored Health Plans, and IRS Publication 502, Medical and Dental Expenses, online, by calling the IRS to request a copy of each at 800.829.3676

I also found an online site www.hsasearch.com to help you find an HSA administrator and compare fees and investing options. I'm sure you can google health savings account and find other such sites as well."

"For what it's worth, let me pitch in here," says Doug, and all eyes shift to him. "I opened an HSA account at my company, and I have my contribution deducted from my pay. And because HSAs are individually owned, it will stay with me if I change jobs or retire." Clearing his throat, Doug continues, "We were told you can use an HSA account for tax-free withdrawals to pay a portion of long-term care insurance premiums with limitations based on your age. After you turn sixty-five, you can use HSA money to pay premiums for Medicare Part A, B, or D and qualified copays for Part D. Medicare Advantage, Medicare HMO, and MAPD plan premiums are also eligible expenses for reimbursement and long-term care insurance premiums. Of course, the educational material indicated to consult your tax advisor."

Jodi sums it up. "I am pleased we have HSA accounts. It is certainly a very useful tax efficient funding mechanism that we will incorporate into creating a financially stable retirement plan."

CHAPTER 24

What Are the Options for the Healthy and Not-So-Healthy?

> "Wealth is not about having a lot of money; it's about having a lot of options."
>
> — CHRIS ROCK

So far, the CPT has reviewed four funding options:

- The reliability of depending on Social Security benefits as a major source of income for funding care,
- The desirability of segmenting a large sum of funds for the payment of long-term care expenses,
- The instability of relying on invested funds for payments, which could lead to unfortunate market timing and tax implications,
- And the advantages of using HSA account money to help fund insurance policy premium payments.

Having examined those options, at the next CPT meeting, the group is ready to looks at additional options with the objective of ensuring their personal preferences are met without destroying lifestyles or family ties.

For someone in good or relatively good health, insurance options include:

- Traditional long-term care insurance
- Worksite group long-term care insurance
- Whole and universal life insurance
- Life insurance with riders
- Annuities with riders
- Term insurance with riders

For someone with some health issues or budget concerns, insurance and noninsurance options include:

- Short-term care insurance
- Reverse mortgages
- Life settlements

For impaired health cases, insurance and noninsurance options include:

- A single premium immediate annuity (SPIA) or a Medicaid Compliant Annuity
- Veterans benefits
- Medicare (benefits are limited)

For someone who meets the definition of impoverished, noninsurance options include:

- Medicaid
- State and County services

"Wow, I'm amazed at the number of available options." Nicole seems both surprised and pleased. "Now I see why you insisted on moving forward with the three steps. Compared to our grandparents, this is a whole different ball game."

Jodi replies, "True! And we will have help. Our advisor is a member of the National Association of Insurance and Financial Advisors, or NAIFA. It's a professional organization that provides her with access to specialists who sponsor the NAIFA Limited and Extended Care Planning Center. Additionally, she maintains the prestigious Certified Financial Planner® certification which expands her ability to access additional resources as a member of the Financial Planning Association (FPA) which has been the premier partner in planning to Certified Financial Planner™ (CFP) professionals and others engaged in the financial planning process. For this CPT, she suggests a basic overview of options and not an in-depth analysis." Smiling, she adds, "We don't want to become paralyzed by information overload; we just want to become educated consumers."

Jackson, indicating himself and Jodi, adds, "And learning isn't just for our benefit. Once you expand your knowledge base, when you do meet with an advisor or agent, you can explain the direction you may want to go, dig into details with your advisor or at the very least ask good questions."

Nicole smiles. "Perfect!"

Becoming familiar with options in order to effectively plan is a perfect step, but there is no such thing as a perfect solution. Underwriting, product availability, state requirements, cost, and riders which are add-on benefits or options, company ratings, etc., may impact the selection. In addition, postponing or not moving ahead with a plan may result in you being ineligible for a plan option that would have fit your needs and budget, if you had acted earlier.

There is a popular saying in the long-term care insurance business: Your health buys you insurance; your money just pays for it. Over a relatively short period, numerous extended and long-term care options have developed and are continuing to develop and evolve to serve numerous health and financial situations. There is a right one for you if you take the time to really understand your potential needs, so ask the right questions, and establish a plan.

Jodi and James make a list of insurance options they want to consider while they are still eligible. The CPT members choose various insurance options to examine.

CHAPTER 25

The Pros and Cons of Traditional Long-Term Care

> "Don't judge a book by its cover."
> — GEORGE ELIOT

The CPT decides to hold the next meeting at Nicole's home since she had a scheduled business call and didn't want to rush over to her parents' place. Once they settle in and grab drinks, Jodi, somewhat familiar with the first option of traditional long-term care since she called out some facts that removed it from consideration for her parents, begins.

"I mentioned this option during my parents' CPT, but Jackson and I are in better health, we are younger, and our finances are still growing—so it's a very different scenario. Traditional Long-Term Care Insurance, or TLTC, may also be referred to as stand-alone LTC. Some advisors refer to it as pure protection since, unlike some other insurance options where policies combine different coverages, TLTC focuses solely on offsetting expenses for a long-term care need. TLTC policies have established benefit triggers and are underwritten for morbidity not mortality."

Nicole reminds her mother, "Mom, remember we said that whoever is presenting should define words the way insurance companies define or use them."

Nicole reminds us of a very important point. As you review products, it's important to understand insurance lingo. Words have different connotations depending on the context in which they are used. Learn the definitions of keywords in the context of the insurance contact so you and the insurer are on the same page.

For example, morbidity is not just feeling gloomy or morbid, which is how most of us define the word. In insurance lingo, morbidity refers to having a disease or a symptom of a disease.

Examples of morbidity include injuries from motor-vehicle accidents, drug poisoning, falls, or violence; other examples include infectious diseases like the COVID-19 virus, other influenzas, food-borne illness, health-care–associated infections, and sexually transmitted infections.

Mortality refers to the state of being mortal or destined to die. In medicine and long-term care insurance, the term is also used for death rate, or the number of deaths in a certain group of people during a certain period.

In terms of traditional long-term care and long-term care riders, benefit triggers under the Health Insurance Portability and Accountability Act of 1996, are defined and used to determine when a policyholder is considered chronically ill and thus eligible for claim benefits. A licensed health-care practitioner must certify that the insured:

- has a severe cognitive impairment that requires continual supervision to prevent them from harming themselves or others, or

- is unable to perform without substantial assistance from another individual at least two activities of daily living (ADL) for at least ninety days due to a loss of functional capacity. The activities of daily living are bathing, continence, dressing, eating, toileting, and transferring (for example, getting out of a bed and into a chair).

Jodi continues, "Many consumers and advisors still consider TLTC a solid option because TLTC policies typically offer more comprehensive coverage and there is usually a good deal of benefit design flexibility."

Doug observes, "Sounds like TLTC could be the foundation for a good extended or long-term care plan. I think I've heard about an issue."

Doug brings up another important element of an overview; pairing up the good with the not-so-good issues that may be attached to a product. In the case of TLTC, unfortunately, older policies have incurred the ire of the press and the public due to increased premium payments. They rarely mention the billions the industry has paid out in claims.

Doug explains, "One of my buddy's parents got rate increases on their policy. They weren't happy!"

"What did they do about it?" Nicole asks.

"They said that the insurance company included alternate premium payment offers in the letter they received about the rate increase. Their agent also received a copy of the letter. They reviewed and discussed the alternate offers together. They opted for one that fit their current situation so they were comfortable keeping the policy. Besides, when they looked at the cost of a current policy or other coverages, it made the increased premium seem pretty decent for the coverage!"

One final tip for increasing the effectiveness of the CPT is to remember to consider non-monetary contract benefits. The more you explore an option—including history and current offerings—the more you will find options that may be right for you. Then, dig in and review pertinent details with a professional.

CHAPTER 26

Worksite Limited, Extended, and Long-Term Care

> "Opportunities are like sunrises. If you wait too long, you miss them."
>
> — WILLIAM ARTHUR WARD

Aside from working individually with an agent, you may be able to buy a policy as part of the supplemental benefits offered through your employer.

The worksite market has expanded to include hybrid/combo/linked sales and individual policies and group certificates sold with discounts and/or underwriting concessions to qualifying groups of people based on common employment. Fortunately, Jackson's friend Doug is able to share his experience with buying LTC at his worksite.

"My previous employer offered worksite long-term care coverage," Doug begins. "I took advantage of the offer, bought a policy, and have the deductions taken right out of my paycheck. I elected to include a three percent inflation benefit on my policy to keep up with increasing medical and care expenses. I am no longer with that employer. I took a different position and moved back here, but the policy is still in force. I now pay the premiums directly. Actually, I have them automatically withdrawn from my bank account. I'm happy to report my maximum daily benefit amount has grown thanks to the inflation benefit."

"So you found the process pretty easy, Doug? Even after leaving that particular employer, they didn't drop you?" Erik asks.

"Nope. I brought a clipping for tonight's session from a Transamerica Retirement Center survey of workers. Twenty-eight percent of workers are currently serving and/or have served as a caregiver for a relative or friend during the course of their working career. Current research about the impact of being an employed caregiver foretells an alarming future reality that may very negatively impact not only us but generations above and beneath us as well."

"I didn't qualify for a promotion due to caring for my parents," Jodi admits. "Along with financial repercussions, I certainly experienced fallout at work and emotional stress at home. Now my parents have a funded plan in place, I'm no longer continuously stressed and dreading personal or professional consequences."

Worksite programs play a key role in helping employees access long-term care benefits that fit their needs and lifestyles. Purchasing or paying for future benefits at the worksite should involve education and advice. Don't hesitate to ask questions!

CHAPTER 27

Publicly Funded State Long-Term Care Programs

"You have as many options as you give yourself."

— *KASIE WEST*

Erik and Nicole are learning about the advantages of future care planning due to their involvement with the CPT. However, they are also aware of news reports about the unsustainability of Medicaid funding for long-term care recipients.

Nicole comments, "My brother and I came close to experiencing lots of long term, difficult, nonreversible consequences due to our grandparent's care needs. We are two generations younger, but we still felt the impact. I read that the financial consequences of so many people being unprepared for aging and long-term care needs will be felt via state and federal budgets, which will impact all of us financially. I respect that the states must deal with the expectation of inadequate funds for the needs of an aging population, but I am glad I have the opportunity to create my own plan!"

States are actively looking into programs, and in some cases have legislation proposed for publicly funded long-term care programs. Washington State is a first-in-the-nation publicly funded LTC program. Publicly funded, in this context, means financial support in part or in full with revenue generated from workers income.

In 2019, the Washington State legislature passed the LTSS Trust Act (RCW 50B.04) and it was signed into law by Governor Inslee the same year. Renamed the Washington Cares Trust Act/Fund, the program will be supported solely by employees contributions via a premium payroll deducted assessment all on W-2 earnings. Employees who attested they had purchased qualifying long-term care insurance prior to the established November 1, 2021 cut-off date were able to apply for an exemption from the premium assessment. This created a substantial run on the private LTC market, causing many carriers to significantly limit or suspend sales entirely. Starting July 1, 2026, for those meeting eligibility criteria, a onetime benefit of $36,500 can be used to purchase long-term care services which may include professional care, equipment, home safety evaluations, and/or compensation for family members who provide care. Legal, political, and administrative challenges are still being worked out. Individuals should consult their legal or tax professional for specifics and information.

California is among the many additional states considering various legislative solutions to a publicly funded long-term care program. AB 567 (Calderon) established the Long Term Care Insurance Task Force in the California Department of Insurance which began meeting in March 2021. The Task Force's work is part of a larger California "Master Plan for Aging" which was initiated in June 2019 by Executive Order N-14-19 from Governor Gavin Newson. The Task Force is charged with recommending options for establishing a statewide long-term care insurance program and comment on the respective degrees of feasibility of those options in a report submitted to the commissioner, the governor, and the legislature on December 23, 2022. The options submitted by the Task Force undergo a feasibility financial analysis. The resulting Actuarial Report will be submitted to the Legislature by January 1, 2024.

Additional states are in various stages of studying publicly funded LTC programs. Other states have initiated programs to offer support to caregivers. For example, Hawaii has a pilot program, Kupuna Caregivers, which focuses on the caregiver, rather than the care recipient. In addition to state proposals, there are also several Federal proposals.

If you want to be in charge of your limited, extended, or long-term care needs, then now is the time to investigate your options and seek advice.

CHAPTER 28

Whole Life and Universal Life Insurance

> "If you change the way you look at things, the things you look at change."
>
> — WAYNE DYER

After realizing the potential long term effect that a state tax to support a public LTC program could have on their W-2 income, including bonuses and stock options, the CPT increases the frequency of schedule calls. They schedule a series of Zoom calls to continue to look at private LTC funding options.

While traditional and worksite LTC products may be specifically designed to provide coverage for long-term care, whole life and universal life insurance may provide funding. Whole life insurance provides permanent death benefit coverage for the life of the insured. The cash accounts are guaranteed to grow based on insurance company calculations; while in universal life policies, cash grows, depending on type of policy, and current interest rates.

At the start of the call, Jackson reminds the CPT he has a whole life insurance policy, but unlike Grandpa he sees it as an asset as much as a legacy.

"When Mom and I first got married," Jackson says, looking affectionately at Jodi, "I wanted to be sure that if something happened to me, she would have money to support herself and you kids. So, I bought a whole life insurance policy. The cash-value portion of my policy accrues tax-deferred interest, and there's a policy provision that allows me to take a non-taxable cash-value withdrawal up to my policy basis, which is the amount of premiums I've paid into the policy. Mom and I discussed the possibility of using this as an option to pay for unexpected care costs."

Jackson will need to review the policy details with his agent and understand all the pros and cons of this option.

CHAPTER 29

The Hybrid/Combo/Linked-Benefit Marketplace

> "Innovation is the ability to see change as an opportunity -not a threat."
>
> — *STEVE JOBS*

As we move to a discussion about hybrid/combo/linked marketplace products, insurance lingo tends to become even more specialized, if not convoluted. Similar to other emerging product lines, we will have to allow the industry some time to standardize terminology to keep up with product and service innovations.

Currently, each insurer may use one of four product names: combination, linked, asset based, or hybrid. No matter what the product is called, it is important to understand what the product does or does not do in terms of your personal situation and objectives.

The CPT seems willing to tackle the complexity, but start off on a light note! They are pleased Erik can join this Zoom meeting and has been keeping up through the shared summaries. Their banter reminds us that members of the CPT have varying availability, play different roles, have individualized relationships with one another, and exhibit different skill sets.

Erik greets everyone and mentions that Jodi said this topic includes a good deal of detail, adding, "Nicole is the detail person while I prefer the big picture view. That arrangement works really well for us when we deal with parental issues. So, if I don't ask specific questions, it doesn't mean I am lost or not paying attention."

"OK, Erik," Jodi says, her tone serious while her face reveals her amusement. "Dad and I respect your division of labor! Speaking of a division, here is how I suggest we divide up this more complex topic. We will schedule a series of four calls. This call will focus on the foundation and expansion of the hybrid/combo/linked benefit marketplace. Our second call will review life insurance riders, and our third call will focus on annuities to which riders can attach. The fourth call will focus on various health related riders currently available to pair up with various products."

"Sounds good," Erik says. "So, why did carriers create these types of policies since there are traditional long-term care policies still available?"

Good question! Even though newer TLTC policies are less susceptible to premium increases, they still don't address one of the most frequent objections which is if you don't need long-term care, you forfeit all the money you paid in premiums. Some traditional long-term care policies offer a return-of-premium rider, but the rider can be rather expensive.

In response to the reality of the marketplace, some insurers create products with guarantees while others incorporate flexibility in their plan design and investment opportunities. Younger individuals have longer investment horizons and may want to take advantage of market growth potential. Insurers are responding with products that speak to lifestyle and investment opportunities.

Jackson remarks, "My understanding is carriers are creating these types of policies that combine two types of insurance products in response to consumer demand and a desire to broaden the marketplace since these newer iterations of policies may provide more people coverage that works with their objectives."

Nicole, with a touch of disapproval in her tone, says, "Well, you would think that seeing and hearing in the news what's on the horizon with local and global illnesses, an aging population, and the overwhelming difficulty of finding qualified staffing for hospitals and other facilities, homemaker aides, first responders, and emergency services that everyone would certainly be open to at least a discussion about how to plan for themselves and those they care about!"

Jodi and Jackson exchange a quick look conveying an unspoken comment about the kids not initially being ready to jump back into planning!

Doug covers his friends by remarking, "It's good that insurers are creating products that can serve a wider swath of Americans."

Even though some of the newer products may have similar names, remember one important rule: look at the words as defined in the policy to understand what the policy actually provides or excludes. The term combination, or combo, product is generally an umbrella term that may include LTC riders on life insurance, linked-benefit LTC, and annuity-based LTC coverage and sometimes chronic illness riders on life insurance. The term rider denotes an additional benefit added to an insurance policy that may specify an additional premium payment. Riders customize insurance policies to address specific needs or budgets.

There are significant differences in products, which is why I advise you to take a deep dive with a specialist after the CPT overview helps you determine a direction that fits your situation. Remember, the name is not the determinate factor; the contract is.

Checking back in with the CPT, we see they are quickly absorbing the basics.

Doug has a playful sparkle in his eyes as he says, "Are these sometimes called twofers? Jackson and I were watching the game the other night with friends and we mentioned we were looking into some policies for extended care coverage. One of our buddies said, 'Oh, are you considering a twofer?' At first we thought he had switched topics and was talking about betting on the game!"

Enjoying Doug's story, Jackson adds, "He told us that twofers refer to a contract that covers more than one risk; in this case, it refers to a policy that offsets some of the extended or long-term care funding risk and the financial impact of death. If care isn't needed, these policies pay a death benefit, or in the case of an annuity, a stream of income payments."

"Thanks for that info. It's good to know your buddy is also looking at off-setting risks." Jodi wraps up the session. "Well, that's our introduction to this growing marketplace. Next week, we will dive into some details on hybrid and linked life insurance policies. Since Doug has offered us a descriptive name for those products, we will let him start things off at our next meeting."

"Yup, right, thanks," Doug says with a pretty audible dose of sarcasm.

CHAPTER 30

What Are Twofers and Double Twofers, and How Can They Help?

> "Ultimately, we have just one moral duty: to reclaim large areas of peace in ourselves."
>
> — ETTY HILLESUM

After greetings are exchanged on the next Zoom call, Doug starts off the CPT conversation by reminding everyone he was assigned the twofer topic. Trying to suppress a smile, he feigns discontentment. "That's what I get for making a joke about such a serious topic."

Jodi throws him a phony reprimanding expression and playfully adds, "The stage is yours, Doug."

"Thanks, Jodi! Twofers, as we now refer to them, are products designed to offset two risks. All riders, which are add-on features, are attached to a base plan and are decided at the time of purchase. Rider pricing is indicated unless there is no charge for the rider. But no charge doesn't make it free. The charge is factored into the total premium costs."

Doug lists the three most common designs of double twofers:

- Life insurance with an LTC accelerated death benefit rider
- LTC + life insurance with an extension of benefits rider
- Life insurance with a chronic illness rider

Not every insurer who offers life insurance offers a long-term care rider, chronic illness, or guaranteed benefit premiums.

Erik, who is a car enthusiast, comments, "It sounds sort of like car manufacturers who create different models on a chassis. They build the base and then you can elect to add different features."

Doug shares Erik's enthusiasm. "Yes, Erik, I like the analogy!"

"It's important to remember that the first and foremost reason that people usually buy life insurance is that at least one person, possibly more, depend on him or her financially. It's also used in business and estate planning designs."

Jackson relates this point to his own situation. "That means if you absolutely need the life insurance to be in place as part of family protection, a legacy, as part of spousal protection in retirement, or business continuation planning, that consideration may mean that, initially, someone may not select life insurance as the base product where the death benefit is diminished by the living benefit. Since I already have life insurance in place, that isn't a major concern for me."

"So here comes the part where I explain why they are twofers," Doug continues. "The death benefit is designed to take care of loved ones when the insured dies, but—and this is important—the living benefit is designed to avoid negative consequences for loved ones, if the insured doesn't die but needs care."

"So, Doug," Nicole restates for clarity, "twofer policies cover two risks, one being premature death and the other being the financial impact of extended care needs. Those certainly help family and friends. But, Doug, they are really double twofers. Let me explain."

She continues. "Let's say that I am married and have children."

Everyone raises their eyebrows in unison. Erik asks, "Is this an announcement of your pending marriage?"

"Not yet, dear brother," Nicole responds while blushing. "Anyway, let's just imagine that I am married. First, as Doug pointed out, the policy helps avoid certain unwanted consequences for my family via the death benefit. Second, the policy provides funding so my family members or friends don't forcibly become caregivers or stop saving for their own retirement. Those are substantial advantages for my family. However, there are also two additional benefits for me as the insured. The third advantage of these policies is they provide me control over my personal care decisions via funding." Nicole briefly pauses.

"Fourth, the policy provides me dignity and diminishes the stress of feeling like a burden to my family. So, they are actually double twofers!"

Everyone appreciates the dramatic delivery, rather unusual for Nicole.

Doug happily concedes, "Double twofers. I love it, Nicole!" Smiling, he moves on with the product overview. "Let's take a closer look at these twofers. Let's start with life insurance with a long-term care acceleration death benefit (ADB) rider. If there is a qualifying long-term care claim, money paid out for the claim reduces the death benefit the beneficiary would be entitled to receive. If long-term care services are not needed or if all the death benefit is not used up to pay for long-term care expenses, the remaining death benefit is paid out to the beneficiaries upon the death of the insured."

Nicole asks, "If someone exhausts the entire available death benefit offered by the ADB rider, what happens if they still need care?"

"Excellent question! One that insurers heard and responded to by creating the next design I will briefly describe," Doug replies. "Let's say, like your Dad, you have life insurance in place. So the focus would be getting LTC coverage. But you don't want a traditional policy since you want to be sure to get something in return for premiums paid. In that case, the LTC + life insurance with an extension of benefits (EOB) rider might be a better fit since it might offer two or three times the death benefit in the form of a long-term care pool. Adding an EOB rider means that, unlike the accelerated death benefit (ADB) rider model, LTC benefits may be paid out from a separate LTC pool even after the death benefit has been depleted. In some cases, an inflation benefit can be added to the second pool. It is very important to understand that the second pool, the EOB rider pool, may only be used for long-term care benefits. It does not pay out as a death benefit."

Doug closes the discussion. "That's a wrap since we decided to review the chronic illness riders along with terminal and critical illness riders on a future call."

Jodi thanks Doug and reminds everyone about the time and place for the next get-together. "Nice job, Doug and Nicole! Remember, Nicole, we'll meet at your place and you'll lead the discussion on annuities. Thanks, everyone."

CHAPTER 31

Annuities with Riders

> "Never depend on single income.
> Make investments to create a second source."
>
> — WARREN BUFFET

In a sense, an annuity is like reverse life insurance. Instead of insuring against death, annuities are designed to protect against longevity risk, meaning the risk you will outlive your income and savings.

Basically, an annuity is a contract between you and an insurance company or similar financial institution under which, in exchange for a lump sum or ongoing premium payments, the insurance company agrees to make regular payments for either the rest of your life or for a predetermined number of years.

The CPT decided to meet, once again, at Nicole's home. After chatting about the latest news on Erik's children, Nicole kicks off the meeting. "My topic is annuities. One of the biggest attractions of annuities is that the growth earned on the single sum or ongoing payments isn't immediately taxable. This feature, called deferred growth, means you don't owe any taxes on an annuity's earnings until you actually receive the money. The period in which you start receiving money back from the insurance company is known as the annuitization phase. When an insured takes an annuity withdrawal to cover costs associated with long-term care needs, he or she deals with the associated ordinary income, gains-first tax treatment and pays taxes accordingly. Adding an extended or long-term care rider to an annuity can provide funds for long-term care expenses without exacerbating the tax burden. Without a long-term care rider, normally the annuity pays one monthly benefit amount. But if you ever need long-term care, the annuity with the rider may apply a multiplier resulting in a higher monthly benefit.

There are annuity expenses and fees, including mortality and administrative fees. These charges pay for any insurance guarantees that are automatically included in the annuity and the selling and administrative expenses of the contract."

Looking pleased, Jodi says, "Great summary, Nicole."

An advantage of the CPT is that you can prepare for a meeting with agents/advisors/CPA/tax or legal consultants armed with questions offered by CPT members that you may not have thought of.

Nicole suggests, "For a change of pace, let's compile a list of questions that we might discuss with an agent or advisor."

"Oh, great idea!" Doug kicks the list off, revealing that he is somewhat curious if this option is a serious contender for his friends' coverage. "If you and your spouse both qualify and need LTC benefits, does the LTC rider cover both of you?"

Erik's love of cars comes in handy. "Car insurers offer different discounts when you have multiple vehicles or drivers. Is there a couple's discount?"

Doug offers a second question, "How does the death benefit pay heirs if the policyholder dies and the long-term care benefits haven't been used?"

"My question," Jodi says, "is if I use the EOB LTC benefit for a couple of years and then stop, does the benefit carry over to a second incident if I again qualify?"

"Do you still remember the questions you texted me?" Nicole looks up from her i-pad where she is compiling the list and looks at her father.

"Yup! Are annuities underwritten like life insurance?" Jackson smiles at Nicole. "Don't want to overlook those details!"

Nicole closes the meeting by teasing her dad. "Maybe you should ask, 'Who is a good candidate for an annuity versus a TLTC policy?' I think the next meeting is an overview of annuities for those not in the best of health."

CHAPTER 32

Single Premium Immediate Annuity

> "Success is the process itself."
>
> — MATT DAMON

Many insurers target different health-care needs brought on by different lifestyles, family health history, and financial circumstances. A single premium immediate annuity is designed for income purposes only and may also be called an income annuity, or simply an immediate annuity. A medically underwritten single premium immediate annuity helps fund immediate care needs with monthly payments guaranteed for life. While this income stream may be guaranteed for life, like all extended or long-term care options, it may not cover all costs associated with long-term care.

This type of policy is attractive for someone with a health-related condition, such as heart disease, alcoholism, leukemia, or cirrhosis of the liver, that might shorten their life. The underwriting is unique. Instead of proving you are in good health, the applicant is actually required to provide documentation to support their health condition diagnosis. As you might suspect, the insurer may further investigate the applicant's health history, and may include a request that the applicant undergo a medical exam.

What about people who appear to be in good health but whose illness is less apparent? There are plenty of stories about long-term care needs lasting for years, especially in the case of dementia or Alzheimer's disease. Nicole offers a personal story that stuck with her.

"Erik, do you remember my college friend, Adriana?" Nicole asks her brother.

"Sort of, why?" Erik answers.

"Her dad was diagnosed with early onset Alzheimer's disease. For a long time, her dad, along with everyone else, just tried to ignore it. She described to me the sadness and the nightmare of when her dad finally admitted he didn't feel quite right. The family began to notice unopened mail, but he hid that he started getting calls from creditors since he was confused about paying bills. Worse, they discovered he had become a victim of scammers. As Mom has pointed out several times, planning for extended care is a tough subject to discuss. I guess the natural instinct is to pretend it would just get better or go away. It doesn't just go away, and they were looking at years of increasing costly care and emotional angst."

"How old was her dad?" Jackson asks. "What did they do?"

"He was young; early sixties. I think they went bankrupt, if not financially, then for sure emotionally. The toll on my friend was huge."

The group is quiet as they process this.

Nicole continues. "After a semester, she took leave to help her mom with her dad. Eventually, they had to find a facility for him. It cut her to the core, not just because she was seeing her dad's mental health deteriorate, but she sort of lost her mom, his caregiver, as well. I don't know how it impacted her future since I don't know if she returned to school or could afford to.

I haven't thought about it for years. I'm not sure what the final outcome for her or her family was. She told me the disease can be hereditary. Hopefully, she put a plan in place for herself, just in case. Instead of covering a limited period, I think unlimited coverage is probably something she would consider."

Jackson looks at Doug. He knows Doug is having issues with his father-in-law. "Wow, you hear about these types of situations, but the tendency is to push those thoughts away and just hope it doesn't happen in your family."

Jodi sighs. "Between accidents, long-lasting illnesses, debilitating diseases, Alzheimer's disease, and other forms of dementia on the increase, it is safe to say that services and especially professional and supportive personnel for care needs are going to be pushed beyond the limit. While technology is racing to help with monitoring care, support nurses, doctors, and facility staff, help will probably be in short supply and expensive. And then, like Grandpa, some people find technology aids invasive, which can limit their effectiveness."

It's often difficult to get a parent, sister, brother, close friend, etc., to discuss and feel empowered to find a solution that fits with their health and possible care needs.

CHAPTER 33

How Riders Can Help with Specific Care Needs

> "Extra! Extra! Read All About It!"
> — FRANK SHEERIN

As the industry engages in developing products in response to marketplace demand, they must meet established regulatory, legislative, and tax code requirements. Employing different sections of the IRS code, insurers have developed riders. An insurance rider — also referred to as a floater or an endorsement — is an optional add-on to an insurance policy which are responsive to specific care needs.

Doug asked if the next week's meeting could be a Zoom call. Everyone connects and is chatting. Let's join the CPT call in progress.

Critical Illness and Terminal Illness Riders

Jackson suggests that they start the overview and announces, "Terminal illness riders, critical illness riders, and chronic illness riders are my assignment. Critical illness insurance was developed in 1996, as people realized that surviving a heart attack or stroke could leave them with insurmountable medical bills. Critical illness insurance provides additional coverage for medical illnesses or emergencies like heart attack, stroke, or cancer. It's fair to say critical illness riders are more responsive to immediate needs as opposed to chronic or long-term care needs."

"For me, it's pretty easy to distinguish between terminal illness and critical illness," Nicole says. "A couple of months ago, Erik told me a sobering story about his friend Pete. Pete's mom became critically ill. She had a stroke that resulted in her needing additional physical therapy and medical treatment. He said they were relieved that at least it wasn't a terminal illness diagnosis, which would have meant his mom's illness would lead to death within six to twenty-four months."

"I remember being very shocked by his mom's sudden illness," Jodi adds. "It came out of nowhere. She always seemed like such a healthy person. We used to go to the same gym. Hopefully, they have critical illness insurance to help with the bills."

Chronic Illness Rider

Jackson continues, "It would be wonderful to think of Erik's friend's situation as a one-off. But, that's not the case. Chronic illnesses are on the rise in the United States. A chronic illness can generally be defined as a condition with no medical cure, such as heart disease, certain cancers, Parkinson's disease, or multiple sclerosis. Chronic illnesses create an ongoing need that may last for years. Traditionally, policies offering chronic illness (CI) riders only paid accelerated death benefit payments for a qualifying permanent condition. Many of the newer contracts have removed the requirement. We would have to have our agent check out this detail in the actual contract if we went in that direction.

Before consulting our tax advisor, we would also ask our agent under which Internal Revenue Code the rider is filed since there are differences in the tax treatment depending on which section of the code applies. Aside from that important distinction, other differences surface when examining actual contract language. LTC rider regulations require that consumer protection provisions be included. CI riders are not required to include them, although some do."

Jackson closes the call indicating that the CPT will move onto an overview of limited care options in the next meeting.

CHAPTER 34

Limited-Term Care Options

> "It is better to do something than to do nothing while waiting to do everything."
>
> — *WINSTON CHURCHILL*

Short-Term Care Policies

A short-term care policy is a great option for someone who has health and financial concerns that make other options out of reach; but who still needs/wants coverage. One of our CPT members finds himself in such a situation.

Doug asks Jackson if he can meet him to grab a coffee. They settle into a corner of the café. Doug thanks Jackson for meeting him, explaining that he doesn't want to discuss this at home since it's about his father-in-law. He doesn't want to upset his wife.

"I envy you, Jackson. You got your in-laws settled into a plan to deal with the pressures of their extended care needs."

"Thank goodness! What's on your mind, Doug? You look worried."

Doug asks, "Do you know if there is anything for someone who won't consider any of the insurance options we've already discussed?"

Jackson is clearly surprised. "He won't consider any options that we discussed with Jodi's parents? Did you review government programs or using the home as an asset to access income?"

Doug shakes his head. "They rent their place. He has some savings and modest income but won't consider government aid. And my wife refuses to push him, although she knows her dad is going to need care. I suspect this won't be a case of long-term care, but he isn't really prepared for the cost of care services. I worry about where the money will come from." With a distressed look, Doug admits, "It's already causing a lot of family issues. Hopefully, the CPT will uncover an option that will help and I can get my family to see how helpful it is to work through the steps."

Jackson reassures his friend with an encouraging thought, "We thought my father-in-law would never even discuss care but as a family project, using the steps, he did! Actually, Jodi is presenting Short Term Care tonight. Maybe that might work."

Early that evening, Jodi greets the CPT members and notices Doug's concerned demeanor but decides to say nothing. "Let's get started. A Short Term Care policy, or STC, is generally available for individuals between ages fifty and eighty-nine to cover gaps in I coverage or as an alternative to long-term care protection. This type of policy is sometimes referred to as a recovery care policy. This is a viable option for someone who refuses to even consider going through underwriting other than to answer a few questions or is older than the cutoff issue age for other policy options and/or has limited funds.

"There are other advantages to these types of products which are available both on an individual and worksite basis.

Aside from providing needed limited care protection, someone considering a longer elimination period to lower the cost of a traditional LTC policy may use a STC policy to provide some funding while waiting for the TLTC benefits to kick in. Piggybacking the two policies, STC and TLTC, may also allow the insured to stretch out a TLTC by delaying the start of TLTC benefit payments."

Jodi makes note that the look on Doug's face is brightening. She wraps up the overview, "Most short-term care insurance policies have limited benefit periods less than one full year, but some may provide a benefit for each site of care, meaning benefits may be provided for up to three years. STC is not available in every state. There are significant differences between TLTC and STC. For example, unlike LTC, STC insurance pays in addition to Medicare."

Jodi is tempted to ask Doug about what's on his mind. Instead, she engages in the group's conversation before ending the meeting.

Doug's involvement in the CPT has morphed from passive participant to active beneficiary. He will further investigate STC for his father-in-law. STC is not the only limited-term option available. For younger clients or price-sensitive clients who want to go the twofers route, term insurance may present a good option.

Term insurance with an Accelerated Death Benefit Endorsement Rider

Term life insurance is simple to understand. If premiums are paid, it guarantees payment of a specified death benefit to the insured's specified beneficiaries if the insured person dies during a specified term. Riders can also be added to term insurance. The most common include guaranteed insurability, accidental death, waiver of premium, family income benefit, child term, and return of premium riders. But the one that will interest a younger member of the CPT is an accelerated death benefit endorsement.

Erik texts his mom, "Is there a convenient evening for a call with you and Dad once we get the kids to bed? I probably need additional life insurance now that we have a second child and I am about to celebrate another birthday."

Erik is a typical Gen Xer coveting and enjoying the latest and greatest technology advances. Many of his young children's toys and learning tools connect to apps and remote control devices. As the sole breadwinner of his family, Erik works hard. After accepting a promotion, he moved further away from his parents and bought a new home.

> Jodi sets a date and time but is concerned about discussing Erik's planning need with Jackson. Over dinner the next evening, Jodi feels it would be wise to remind Jackson that while the CPT discussions about family and financial protection has led Erik to want to protect his own family, Jackson needs to remember not to get dictatorial or overly protective. Jackson clearly loves his children, but sometimes he forgets they are now grown adults. Their life experiences, which formed a good deal of their personalities and reactions to planning, are different from her husband's. In planning for themselves, the CPT expects Jodi or Jackson to lead the discussion. Pleased the three steps have reminded Erik to move forward with protecting his own family, she wonders if Jackson can turn over the reins. She also knows Jackson is not a big fan of term insurance so that's another concern.
>
> "Jackson, before we get involved in helping Erik with supplementing his life insurance, I think we should remember something."
>
> "What's that?" Jackson looks up from his dinner plate.

"We are part of the Baby Boomer generation."

"And they are not! Got it!"

"I was just reading an article which indicated that three-quarters of Gen Xers have higher family incomes than their parents did at the same ages, but only a third have higher wealth."

"And then there is a tremendous amount of student debt that they have to carry as well," Jackson adds, warming to the subject.

"Where I am going with this is, since this is Erik's deal, we will have to respect him in the same way he did when we were dealing with our planning. He may not want to share financial details with everyone. We come at it from a different vantage point. We will have to actively listen so we don't misunderstand or dismiss his values, lifestyle, or expectations."

"The kids did ask lots of questions as members of our Care Planning Team. But the questions didn't dig too far into our personal finances or health but instead focused on option features," he says.

Jodi reaches over and squeezes Jackson's hand. "We need to do the same for them." You can almost hear her nervous sigh of relief.

At the next CPT meeting, Jodi tells the group that term insurance with an Accelerated Death Benefit Endorsement is up next on the docket. She is met with some blank stares, so she quickly continues. "Some of the newer term polices come with an accelerated death benefit endorsement. An accelerated death benefit is a living benefit that allows the policyholder to access a portion of the death benefit if diagnosed with a qualifying illness."

Remember the devil is in the detail. In calculating this rider attached to a term policy, most benefit formulas incorporate the severity of the illness, actuarial factors for past and future premiums, life expectancy, and type of coverage. Some carriers may terminate the policy if the policyholder accepts payment of the accelerated benefit.

Jodi has a term policy, and her daughter thinks this is where the conversation is headed. "So, Mom, are you considering trading in your current term policy for one with an accelerated death benefit rider, ADBE for short?"

Erik, who Jodi encouraged to join this particular call, jokes, "Are we looking at another formula? Where's my sister?"

Jodi does not share Erik's request about buying term insurance with the others. Instead, Jodi addresses the topic as if she is considering it as one of her options. "Well, yes, we are! It isn't as simple as it sounds. Plus, life insurance pricing is age sensitive and only gets more expensive as you get older, and despite what you may think, I am not getting any younger."

That clever remark brings on all kinds of teasing from the group.

"OK, let's get serious." Jodi tries to keep a straight face as she continues. "Aside from the cost, I would also be concerned that the policy would be in force when I need it for extended or long-term care, which hopefully is a couple of decades away!" Holding up her hand she says, "Keep it together! And there may be underwriting considerations. I don't think my health has changed since I bought my current policy, but maybe it has a little."

The CPT looks as if they are going to burst trying to restrain themselves from further teasing. Jodi waves her finger as a 'don't say it' warning. When she has quiet, she continues. "And finally, replacement starts a new contestability period, which means if I misstate something relevant to underwriting criteria or knowingly commit fraud, the policy is null and void."

That last remark takes the CPT over the top. Dripping with sarcasm and grinning, Erik teases, "Is that a worry, Mom? Funny you would even mention that!"

Now even Jodi is overcome with laughter.

Erik appreciates his parents didn't mention his request for advice to the group. In Erik's case, since he needs additional insurance and money is tight for the young growing family, term insurance with an Accelerated Death Benefit Endorsement rider is a good option. Although he will need to consider converting the coverage at a later date, for the next twenty years or so, as his family grows and passes through different life stages, he double dips on coverages—life and long-term care. He is aware of the risks, but still rides his motorcycle despite his wife's protests.

CHAPTER 35

Indemnity vs. Reimbursement Payouts

"Whatever you do, make sure it makes you happy."

— *ANONYMOUS*

Erik applies for a Term Life insurance policy with an Accelerated Death Benefits Endorsement that aligns both with his needs and budget. The alignment of premium payments and benefit payout methods with your projected short and long-term budget represents another important planning and tax consideration.

Some contracts offer indemnity payouts while others offer reimbursement or a disability model with a fixed benefit and trigger requirement. The most common are indemnity or reimbursement models. Here is a comparison chart pointing out some differences between the two benefit payout methods.

Reimbursement vs. Cash Indemnity Payout of Benefits

	Reimbursement	Cash Indemnity
Eligibility Requirements	The insured is certified as chronically ill, has a plan of care and satisfied the elimination period	The insured is certified as chronically ill, has a plan of care and satisfied the elimination period
Monthly LTC Benefit	Only expenses incurred on qualified services are reimbursed, not to exceed the monthly maximum	Up to 100% of the monthly maximum is paid as a cash benefit. The stated dollar amount of the per diem limitation (guaranteed tax free, benefit, or reimbursed amount) is announced each year.
Monthly Bill & Receipts	Required	Not required
Informal Care	Limited or no coverage	Yes
Restrictions on Use of Benefits	Limited to qualified LTC expenses incurred as defined in the contract	None

Courtesy LTCI Partners, LLC http://www.ltcipartners.com Steve Cain, steve.cain@ltcipartners.com (608) 283-6600

The upside of a reimbursement method is that once you are approved for benefits, you receive a benefit equal to the total cost of qualified services, up to the policy's predetermined maximum. Since these costs are tied to the actual cost of benefits, there is no tax implication for monies received.

The downside of the reimbursement method is that if the care expenses exceed the monthly benefit, there could be out-of-pocket costs. Your financial plan should include provisions for you to fund the potential balance yourself.

The indemnity method provides monthly payments of a fixed amount, regardless of incurred care costs. The downside is that the pool of money may be exhausted more quickly and there may be a tax implication.

CHAPTER 36

Financial Wellness

> "Nothing in life is to be feared. It is only to be understood."
>
> — MARIE CURIE

Getting The Best Outcome from Assets You Own

For so many of us, life is busy, and we often do not readily have an overall picture of our financial assets and obligations. The CPT accesses the questionnaire on thecaringconversation.com website to kick-start budget priorities and concerns.

> Erik is chatting with his detail-oriented sister. They review the effect on his budget if he adds the term policy with the ADBE rider. At the end of that discussion, he adds, "I accessed that questionnaire on thecaringconversation.com website. The list included questions about 401(k)s. Honestly, I have been so busy I haven't even thought about the one I left with my previous employer. I guess I should add it to my to-do list before I forget about it."

"I get it," says Nicole. "You need to focus on the present and that's a lot! But retirement saving is part of a good plan. Let me pitch in. I'll arrange a call for you and my advisor. He can at least let you know what your options are. Then, you can decide what works best for your family. It's smart not to lose track of previously earned savings and investments."

Nicole's advisor texts Erik and they arrange a call. "Hello, Erik. My name is Joe. Your sister let me know that you have some questions about a 401(k) that you left at your previous employment. First, let me start by complimenting you for contributing to your 401(K) plan."

"My understanding is that you and your wife are now using an online tool to keep yourselves up to date on where you're spending money and what will be set aside for savings. That is a great first step in financial preparedness. I also understand that the immediate issue you want to discuss is whether you should move your 401(k) savings from a prior employment to an IRA account."

"Here is how I suggest we approach this. We'll review the underlying funds expense ratio plus the plan sponsor fees, investment options, etc. to determine if it's more beneficial to rollover a 401(k) to an IRA or to keep the 401(k) with your previous employer."

Joe meets with Erik and his wife to make sure they can articulate and understand their investment goals and risk tolerance before he makes a recommendation.

Topics and conversations which may seem unrelated to extended or long-term care planning can be a catalyst to overall improved financial wellness and retirement planning.

Repositioning Assets

Getting the best possible financial outcome from the assets and insurance contracts that you already own is simply smart. While Erik may move his 401(k), Jackson will consider repositioning his current life insurance policy.

After a short delay in meeting since Jodi needed to spend some time helping her parents, the CPT resumes meeting. This time, they meet at Jodi and Jackson's home. Since Jackson owns a whole life insurance policy that has built up a good deal of cash, he volunteers to offer a quick summary about exchanging the policy under Section 1035 exchange as opposed to borrowing against the cash value if he needed funds for long-term care.

Jackson shares with the group. "I could pull money out of his whole life policy to pay for care but the distribution, above the premiums I've paid into the policy, would be taxable. Or, I could consider using a provision in the IRS code, specifically, Section 1035 which allows for a tax-free transfer of an existing annuity contract, life insurance policy, long-term care product, or endowment for another one of like kind. I may consider exchanging my current life policy for a life insurance policy with LTC rider."

"However, and don't you dare tease me like you did Mom," Jackson warns, "there are also reasons why exchanging my existing policy for a new one may be challenging. There could be underwriting criteria to satisfy, fees, including commissions, a surrender charge, other expenses, higher pricing due to the change in my age or health, a new contestability period during which the insurance company could challenge a death claim based on a material misstatement on the application."

Doug has listened quietly to his friend's presentation. With a broad grin on his face, he says to Jackson, "Well, if you are serious about this exchange, the first call you better make is to our old pal, our tax advisor."

Sometimes friends, like Doug, provide an important direction when we are sharing information. Too often, the topic of extended and long-term care is avoided as too personal among friends. However, this book provides a good opportunity to share a number of stories. Each individual can find themselves or someone they love in these pages. Jodi hesitated to share the burden of caregiving with her own family, and even with a friend in need.

Jodi meets a longtime friend for coffee. She notices that her friend looks worn out. She knows her story. Her friend's parents were unprepared for a long-term care event. It just tore their family apart. She felt guilty that, at the time, she was not more helpful. It's such a tough subject to address. Although her own family was moving towards planning and peace of mind by using the three steps, Jodi had just listened quietly and didn't offer her friend any advice. She didn't want to sound like a know-it-all, or worse, judgmental.

Noticing how more relaxed and healthier Jodi looks, her friend asks, "You look great! You must have a secret about how to handle being the parent to your parents."

"We discovered three basic steps to start the conversation, and importantly, to continue without actually lecturing anyone or making my parents feel as if they are a problem to be handled. I suggest you and your brother try it. Makes you feel saner."

Her friend is desperate. "I'll talk to my brother about it. Somehow, he seems to think that the help and funding my Mom's care needs will just fall out of the sky."

"You sound angry," Jodi responds honestly. "Maybe consider that he simply may not know about a more workable option?"

Her friend, to Jodi's surprise, considers the possibility, but then flatly states, "Well, we'll see if he, or for that matter, his wife will consider discussing options."

Jodi continues to encourage her friend, "Maybe letting them know about the three steps will lead them to see there are affordable, workable approaches or alternatives."

Her friend's tone reveals some bitterness, "Even if we only do a couple of the steps, maybe I will feel more in control and able to get some help. After all, we still have our aging father to worry about. I'm not at all sure our relationship will survive another difficult, stressful situation."

"Don't feel bad, I tried to do it all on my own too. Thank goodness my kids pointed out what it was doing to me and generations above and beneath me. After reviewing various options together, we consulted with several specialists, and to everyone's relief, we got things planned out."

Conceding the relationship with her friend's brother and his wife is already strained, Jodi quickly adds, "You may need to seek an advisor to run through a list of options if family tensions are running too high. That way, it is a third party carving a path to sanity. We were lucky that each of our CPT members wanted to participate and contribute."

"Your CPT? What's that?"

Jodi air hugs her friend. "Get the book, How Not To Pull Your Family Apart. You'll see."

CHAPTER 37

On Becoming an Educated Consumer

"We are stronger when we listen, and smarter when we share."

— *RANIA AL-ABDULLAH*

Feeling grateful to the CPT members for all the research and dialogue to help them plan for potential extended care needs in conjunction with their retirement funding budget, Jackson and Jodi sit down with a couple of glasses of wine and narrow down their choices so they can engage their advisory team. They have almost completed the three steps.

As better-educated consumers, with a grasp of current budget and future monetary obligations, how and where they want to receive benefit payments, health underwriting considerations, pertinent product questions, and personal opinions about product and service preferences, they are ready to move forward!

Narrowing Down Options to the Best Fit

Although it took a couple of evenings to select which options interest each of them, and after consulting with various advisors, Jodi and Jackson are ready to share their choices with the CPT. They invite everyone to dinner. After dinner, Jodi starts off the review. "Somewhat like what your grandparents did before sharing with their entire Care Planning Team, we narrowed down our choices."

"As for self-funding, if you recall, we used a website to estimate current and future costs-of-care. We do not want to keep a large portion of our investment portfolio locked up and dedicated to the possibility of one or both of us needing extended care. Worse, we worry that even a large sum may be quickly depleted, leaving the other person in a bad way."

Jackson takes over, "We feel that underwriting isn't an issue for either of us. We are still young enough to build some equity in a product, and we like the deferred taxation aspect of deferred annuities with LTC riders. Our broker mentioned there is one insurer that offers a discount for two insureds who buy a policy together. So thanks to whoever listed that as a question when we were formulating them."

"Doug is right, I need to have a conversation about a Section 1035 exchange with our tax advisor. I want to see about loaning the cash value built up in my whole life insurance policy versus the 1035 exchange. We'll consult with both our tax advisor and our agent since that will take some analyzing!"

Jodi adds, "We're also interested in pricing life insurance hybrids versus traditional long-term care insurance policies. Alternately, I'm interested in a term policy with an Accelerated Death Benefit Endorsement."

Jackson wraps up, "We'll call our advisor and our broker and ask for some quotes and dig into the details."

Judging from everyone's expressions, it is evident the entire CPT is pleased with the results. Erik offers a toast, "Here's to the freedom that comes with planning."

Nicole chimes in, "For every generation of our family."

Doug raises his glass, "And for a friend who is grateful for all he learned and is now able to help his family consider planning options as well."

CHAPTER 38

Advisors as Moderators, Facilitators, or Mediators

> "I learned a long time ago that there is something worse than missing the goal, and that's not pulling the trigger."
>
> — MIA HAMM, AMERICAN SOCCER PLAYER

Nowadays, so many of us turn to friends and influencers for advice and recommendations. In order to best utilize what you learned from the Jones family's use of the three steps and stories, personalize what you suspect would work for your situation and then seek an advisor/tax consultant/eldercare attorney or other specialist.

Each generation can employ the steps according to their own timeline, finances, historic and current health, and view of the world. When seeking advice, most families will interact with several categories of advisors who all serve different roles. Remember, the devil is in the details so ask lots of questions.

To get a general feeling for Jodi and Jackson's understanding of what works for them, their advisor used a chart that reviewed some pros and cons of various insurance options.

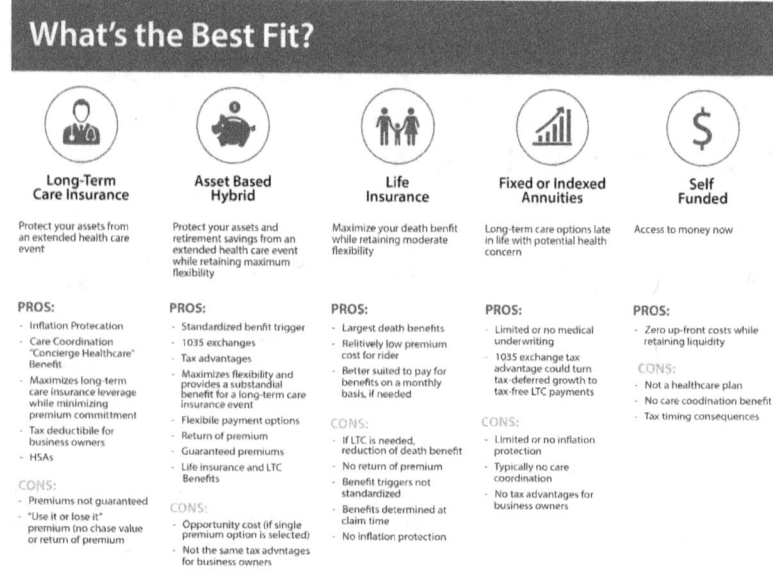

After consulting their tax advisor, final selections were made and policies applied for were issued, Jodi sent a bottle of celebratory wine to each household. At the next get together at Erik's house, the grandparents, Jodi, Jackson, Doug, Nicole, Erik and his wife and children, toast to the success and peace of mind that comes with the completion of the three steps. The little ones dig into grandma's cupcakes without totally understanding why everyone seems very content and happy.

Jackson raises his glass. "Here's to not having our retirement destroyed by unforeseen costs or worrying about becoming a burden to each other or to any of you!"

Jodi now looks like a different person from when they first started going through the three steps with her parents. She is smiling broadly and adds, "And we gave each other fitness watches as an anniversary gift and an exercise bike as a bonus for successfully completing the steps! Cheers, everyone!"

Erik who made sure to host this meeting has been unusually quiet. He and Nicole have odd expressions on their faces. Jackson thought the redo had become a positive thing. He hesitates but decides to clear the air. "Something wrong? Is there is an issue?"

Nicole says, "Reviewing the options will help Erik and I feel more confident and ask more personalized questions when working with a professional. So, let me thank you for that, for both of us, right now."

Jodi is visibly moved, if not confused, by the unexpected appreciation.

Erik elaborates on the surprising direction of the conversation. "Honestly, Mom, we were not that interested in being part of another CPT after we got Grandma and Grandpa's plan done."

"When you said that you and Dad wanted to redo the three steps to avoid being rushed into a solution that you may not like or want, we felt obligated," Nicole admits with a look of apology. "But we also wanted to be supportive," she quickly adds.

"But at the end of the day," Erik adds, "we all got something out of it."

Nicole continues, "We enjoyed being included, value what we have learned, and now realize what to consider for ourselves. We didn't appreciate what an essential role extended or LTC plays as part of planning for a more secure financial future. Hopefully, using a plan for care is way off in the future, but it may not be. Erik applied for a term policy with an Accelerated Death Benefit Endorsement (ADBE) to protect his family and so his wife doesn't look quite so horrified every time he takes the motorcycle out." Nicole smiles at her brother. "I am considering a double twofer. Of equal importance, the process of discovering various options has helped us relax, take control of our budget and savings, pay attention to positioning assets we already have, and decide what direction we want to go and what questions to ask to get us there."

Jackson, looking at his wife, realizes she is a bit overcome by how much this has positively influenced their entire family. He responds for both of them. "Thank you! Mom and I must admit our motivation was to avoid creating havoc in your lives and, I suppose, in ours as well. Watching the impact on Mom that caring for her parents was having while she was trying to maintain her job, her finances, her sanity, and her health was something we didn't want for you." With a playful tone, Jackson adds, "Being caught in the sandwich generation is not a gift we want to give you kids."

Jackson's quip brings things back to a lighter tone. Faces brighten and everyone is ready to celebrate!

Remember, the only plan you are destined to have is the one you decide to create.

CONCLUDING THOUGHTS AND ENCOURAGEMENT

Thank you for joining me and the Jones family as they tackled the daunting issue of starting the conversation and following the three steps to a successful conclusion. For most of us, the tricky part is that life doesn't stop while you're caught up in caring and juggling. Family life, however you define your family, is dynamic and ever-changing.

If you are not yet caught in the sandwich generation, don't wait until it's too late! Without realizing it, you may slowly assume the role of the on-site, on-call, on-the-side, or on-a-flight caregiver who is untrained, unprepared, and eventually unable to manage all that is expected of you.

For many of us, the idea of a role reversal with someone you love is scary. The role of a family caregiver often requires you give up more than just your lifestyle. You may put your own future financial stability at risk.

The primary objective of the three steps is to offer an easy-to-follow, easily adaptable process. But you must start! My three steps offer you a gateway to conversations to get started and not pull you or your family physically, psychologically, or financially apart.

Caring involves a continuum of tiny and sometimes major changes and adjustments. It is an emotional journey but one you can handle with a plan in place. Use whichever of the three steps works for you, in whatever order; use whatever type or size of CPT or support system you need. Please, just get started! This framework will get you to where you need to be—generationally prepared. Plan. Don't panic!

www.ingramcontent.com/pod-product-compliance
Lightning Source LLC
Chambersburg PA
CBHW071241070526
44583CB00017B/2287